Painting the Year

Deborah Last

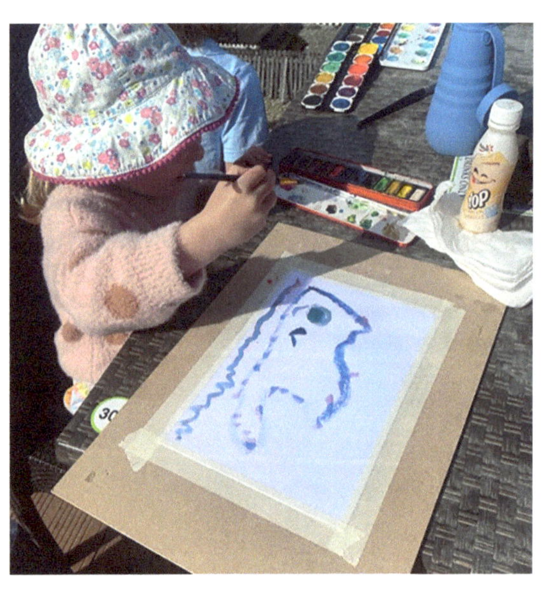
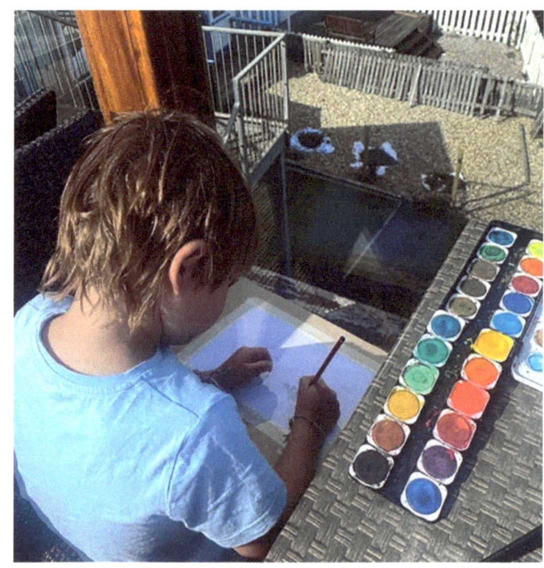

This book is dedicated to my family for being there. I am fully who I am because of you all.

Huge thanks go to Pete for putting up with the project which disrupted and dictated what we did for a whole year! To Kathryn Timms for inspiring me and keeping me going, guiding me round amazing places on Dartmoor, coming out most Tuesdays and for being the unofficial project Chaplain! To Caroline Lumb for joining me and inspiring me on Fridays. To all those in the Monday morning en plein art class for your tenacity and encouragement.

Thanks to everyone cheering me on throughout the project and coming to Pier House Paint Outs. It's been brilliant to do this with others.

This project has been organised and collated by the generosity and determination of Sara Randell without whom I think it might have been impossible to put this book together. Finally an enormous thanks to Nick Hedges for designing and uploading the book and making it everything I had hoped for.

All photos have been taken my myself except for the photos on the back page and my pochade box which are from the Devon Life article and taken by Jim Wileman.

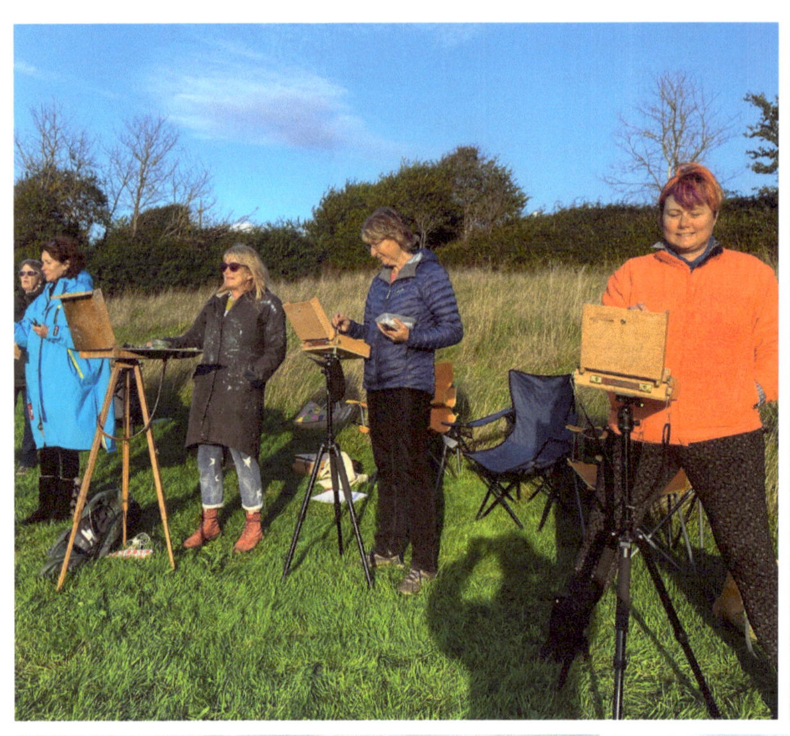
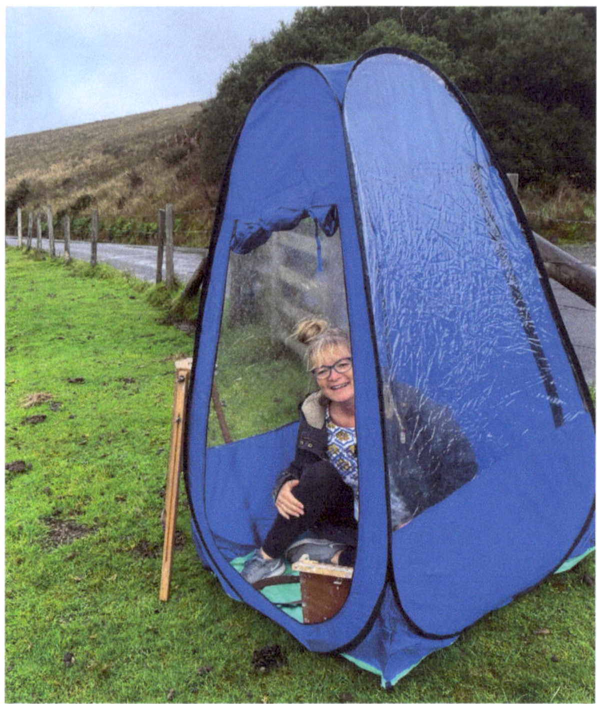
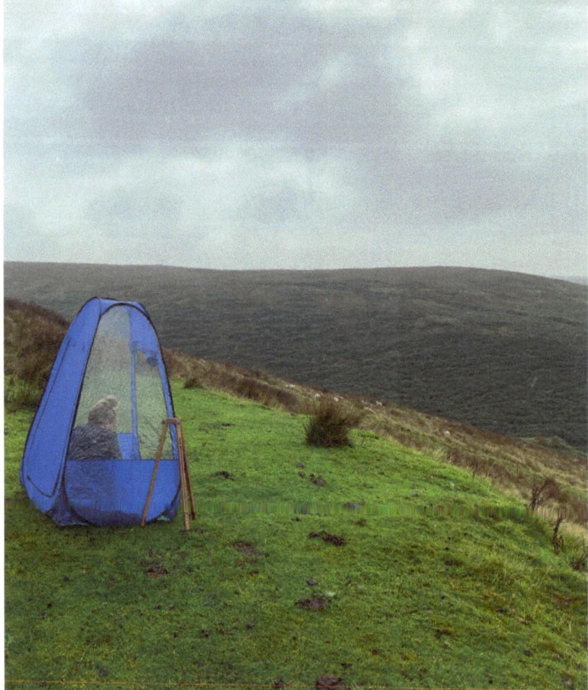
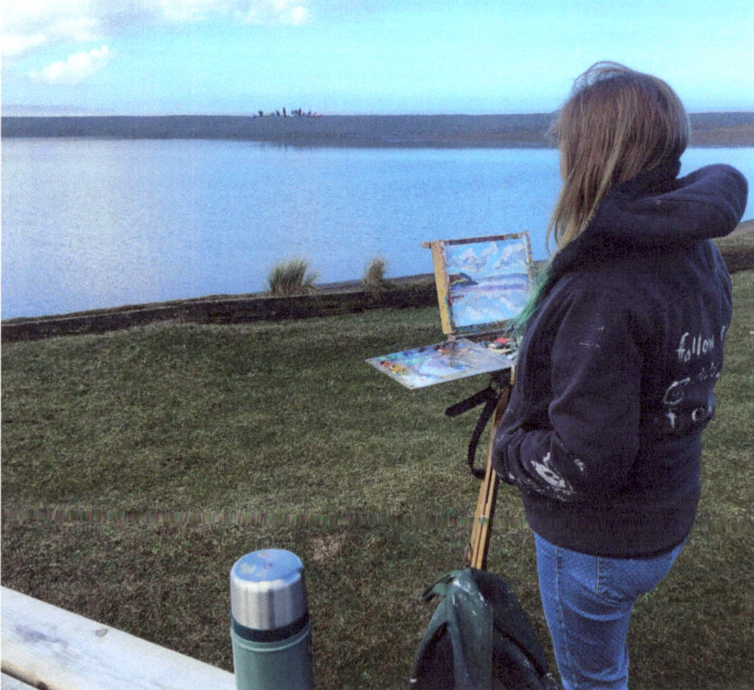

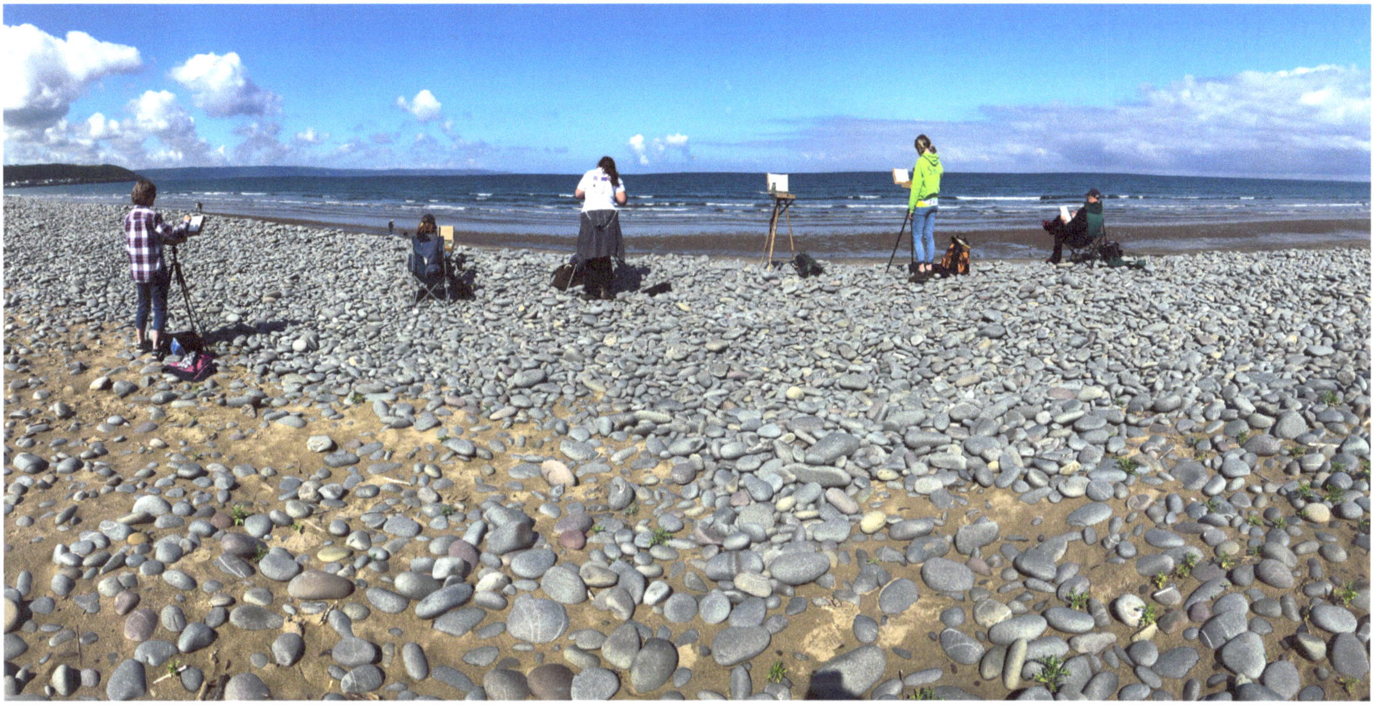

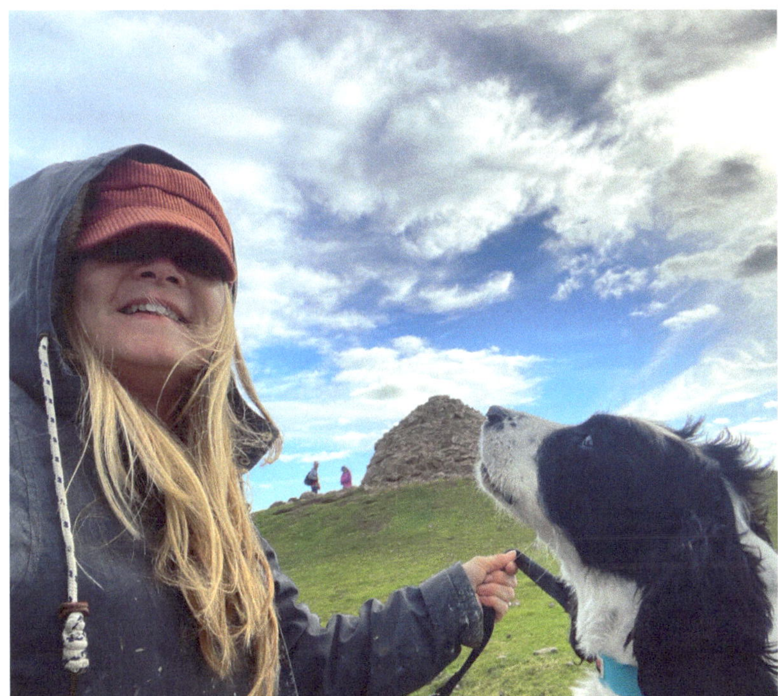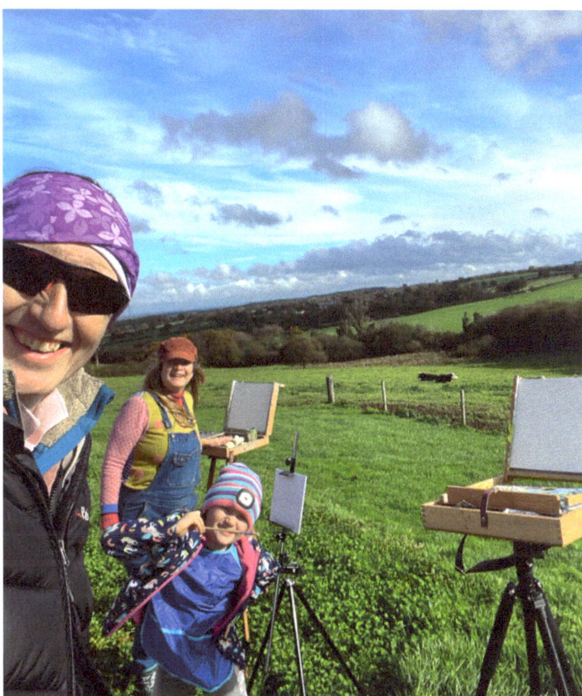

Painting the Year

It's hard not to be inspired by living in a beautiful place like the North Devon biosphere where you are surrounded by breathtakingly beautiful coastlines, dramatic landscapes and so near to both Exmoor and Dartmoor. This was the starting point for beginning the painting the year project.

Throughout 2022, so many people asked me why was I doing this project? Why have you decided to set yourself such a challenge? What is the purpose of painting every day outside for 365 days?

Some days the answer could have been, "I don't know!". On other days the answer was because it was there like some artistic Everest. In reality, there was a sense of doing it a bit better than I had done it previously in 2015 when I painted the landscape every day for a year, but I had not painted them all outside, en plein air. It was also a chance to investigate my practice as a landscape painter and to visually record a year of my life.

I often seem to question why I paint the landscape? It has at times been treated like the poor relation of my artistic endeavours. I think I used 2022 to explore my style and celebrate what it is I love about being in the landscape. The pictures were painted quickly with water-mixable oil and the work has a consistent style that could be considered to be about recording the moment.

On some days the work seems to be looser and bolder in its descriptions and more playful, reflecting my mood and approach at different times of the year. There is a harmony that seems to come from the discipline of the project itself. Perhaps these paintings are as consistent and as freely produced as my own handwriting, with the differences seen depending on the time given to the task and the mood of the day. This challenge was also about a need for a rhythm, a daily practice within my work, something meditative and honouring my practice as an artist.

I painted daily during the pandemic, heading out during the lockdowns once we were able to be outside of our homes. This eased me into the idea of a yearlong project. It was good to be connecting with others who couldn't get outside and bringing the landscape to them through painting. Most of the time I painted it was winter and I developed a system that helped me be outside in all weathers. I gathered my three pochade boxes and the lovely water mixable oils that I like to use and the right clothes, a flask and a rucksack to carry it all in. I worked out how to paint in the car and got myself an angling pod. These things helped me to see that the project was viable and most importantly that a discourse was there to be explored. How do we as humans exist within our environment? Are we better off for connecting with it? Can I do this project and encourage people to join in?

The project has been carefully recorded and each painting is located by What3Words. On the back of each painting a note has been made of the date, the place, who I was with and the What3Words location. Opening the app as I went through the year and watching it fill was a good way to keep going; to see a growing record of what I had done so far.

Also on the back of each painting are the words, Soli Deo Gloria. This is the inscription written by Bach at the bottom of each of his compositions: a reminder that all this might be about acknowledging a higher power and inspiration. It translates as "Solely and only for God's glory". My faith is intrinsic to who I am and is the source of my inspiration. Standing on the heights of Dartmoor a song of joy is often found on my lips. In the days of darkest winter when things seem hard and grey there is a sense that this is all part of the richer tapestry of life, a rhythm of faith and art running together through my life.

At times, I could have thrown in the towel, but as time went on it felt like too much to throw away, each painting having its place in the journey; a record of one year of my life. It was started as an unknown challenge to paint en plein air every day. It felt like many things as it progressed. It was joyful and annoying and at times felt just plain mad. It was great to become collaborative going out each Tuesday with Kathryn Timms and often on Fridays with Caroline Lumb, two wonderful artists and friends. The generosity of their collaboration helped me to keep going with the project often talking through what was going on.

I set up an en plein air class in the September of 2021 to see if it was possible for a class to join me in my project. They were brave and keen to be outside and painted every Monday with me for most of 2022. They braved all sorts of weather even when the wind and the rain seemed to be coming down sideways. The final collaboration I put in place was ending each month at the Pier House in Westward Ho! with a "Paint Out". Lots of people came to this and it was a privilege to paint with people whose work I love and admire and with students and friends turning up just to have a go, helping all this to feel amazing and inspiring which kept me going.

It would have been harder to stop the project once I was a few months in, much harder than carrying on in many ways. I was posting the locations and paintings to Instagram and Facebook every day and this developed an accountability to people following, commenting and cheering me on. It was as though the project wasn't just about me, but was also about those around me and was a record of our lives together. It definitely had an impact on our family life.

At times, our daily lives had to fit around the painting. Sometimes on days off Pete, my husband, sat in the car as I painted out of the back, both of us with a flask of tea and him with a crossword. The pochade box came with me on family days wherever we were meeting up. It came on holiday to Portugal and most notably I painted on our daughter Chloë's and her husband Ross' wedding day in May. The pochade box made a nice little table for champagne glasses once I'd finished!

There were also tough family days like when my Dad had a stroke in September, and I almost felt guilty to go out and paint. I stood on the street where we live and the sky broke into a glorious evening light. I was back from the hospital by then and my mum was safely installed in our house. I knew by then he was going to be okay, and I painted as a thanksgiving that all was well. Also, I felt that Dad might have been sad if his health had been the reason I didn't finish the project.

One of the high points of the project was to be Artist in Residence at Bucks Mills Artist Cabin. This is an amazing, almost magical location on the North Devon Coast. It was a joy painting in this space, where two women artists had painted before and lived their lives; it felt like a wonderful honour to be there.

I was also Artist in Residence for the Appledore Book Festival and used my daily paintings as a record of the week and as part of the creative offer as en plein-air workshops. It was a great week also painting and drawing authors and hearing some wonderful talks.

Painting the year has been a project that has caught the interest of so many people who have watched, encouraged, turned up, come out with me and cheered me along. It has been so good to explore different places, going each month to Exmoor, Dartmoor, Kenwith Reservoir in Bideford and the Pier

House in Westward Ho! North Devon is crammed full of beautiful locations, even doing a painting a day means I have only just begun to scratch the surface of this exploration.

Connecting to the landscape has been so important to me and to so many. The pandemic showed us that so clearly. The paintings span the year; some are strong paintings, given time and headspace whilst others are perhaps less resolved but record the day they were painted on and tell a bigger story than just their own.

It was good to get to the end of the year, exhausting, much more so than I expected but it felt good to have done it and good to be finished. I know it has informed my practice as an artist, it has made me more playful and more experimental and the discipline of using just one media (water-mixable oil) for a whole year has found me being very much more mixed media in my approach in 2023.

Throughout the year there was considerable interest in the project and I was interviewed on a few occasions by BBC Radio Devon who were keen to follow the project. Devon Life also came to photograph my work and interview me whilst I was at Bucks Mills and BBC Spotlight subsequently ran a story about my year, which was wonderful.

This project has been tough and inspiring. I have learned lots about myself as a person and an artist. What started as a rather bonkers New Year's Resolution is now a fully-fledged project.

Enjoy looking at the pictures and perhaps wonder if you too can connect with the landscape or your creativity or both, in some kind of project of your own...

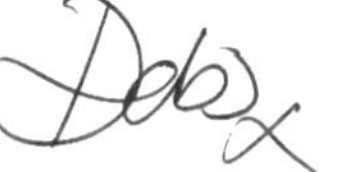

January

I wrote in my morning pages on the 1st of January 2022: "I start the year beginning with this rhythm, daring to paint for the whole of the year, 365 days. Here we come!"

Kathryn, who was to come out nearly every week throughout the year, painted with me on day one. We were in Dolton so that I could see my parents on the first day of the year and we headed to a spot I had been wondering about for a while, thinking it would make a good painting location. It is a roadside garden open for anyone to enjoy. As we checked the What3Words location and the OS map we discovered it was marked as a place of worship. It felt like a good place to be. We prayed, committed the year to God, poured out tea and munched cake... this would be a good way to carry on the year. Painting as a rhythm in the day, as a form of meditation and as a practice and a form of discovery. I was sure at times it would be tough to do this challenge and I wasn't wrong, but as I started I felt even at that moment that I would do it, that I could paint outside every single day of the year for 365 days.

30/01/22
Kenwith Reservoir, Bideford
/// meal.amount.activism

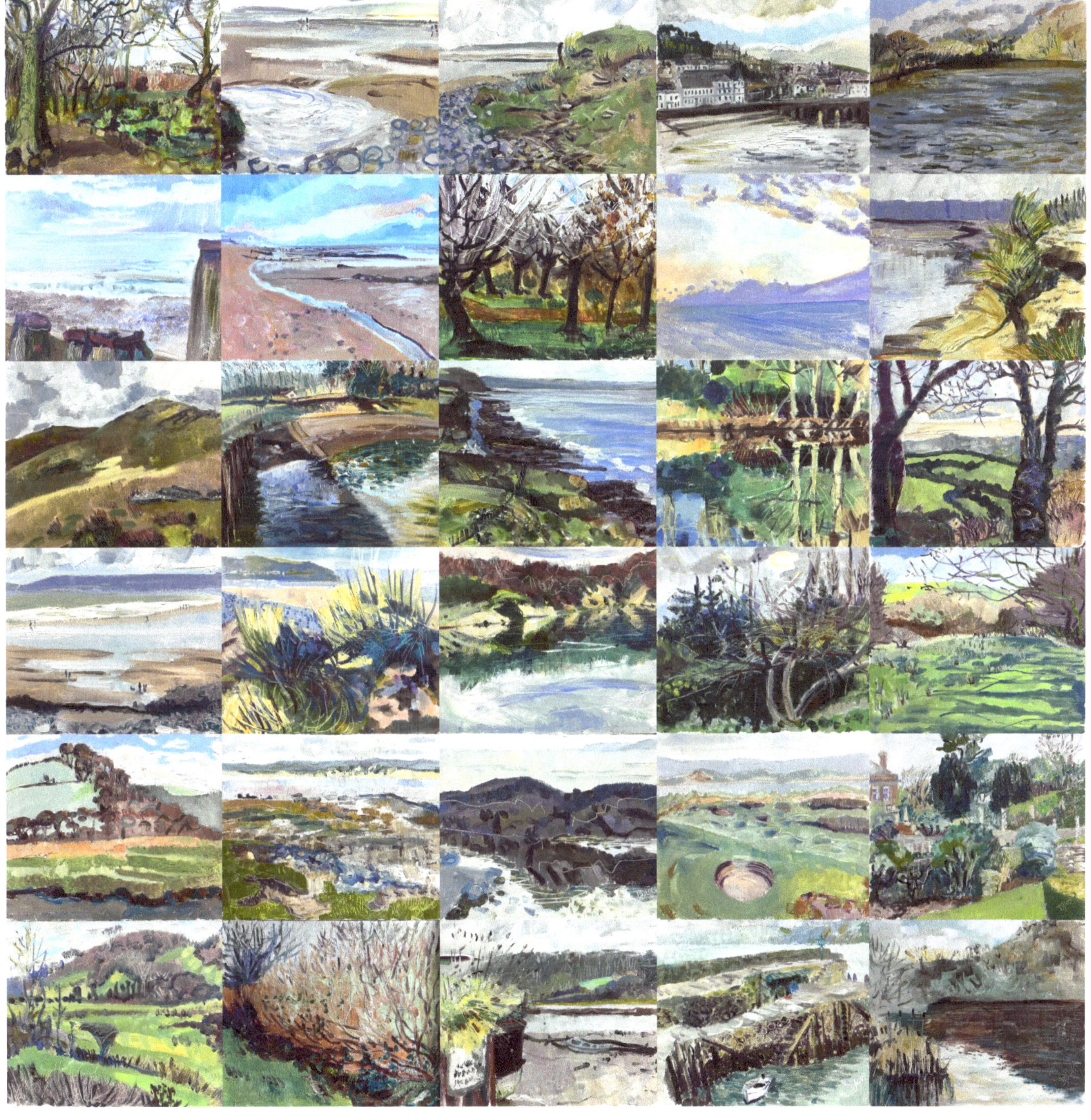

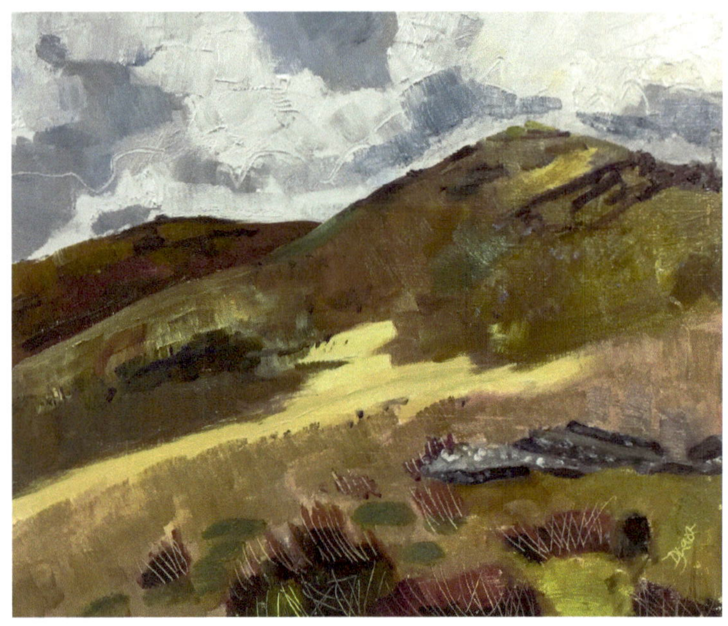

11/01/22
Hangingstone Hill
/// crumbles.price.abruptly

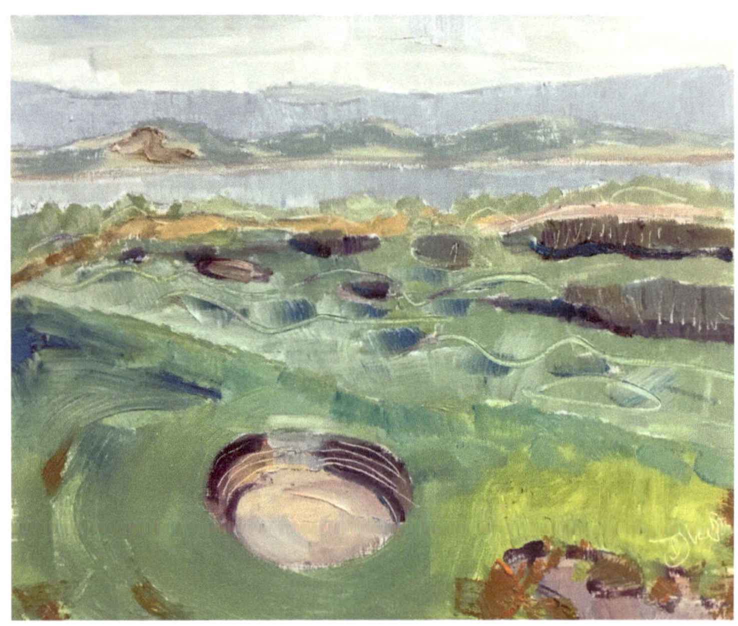

24/01/22
Royal North Devon Golf Club
/// rings.renting.increment

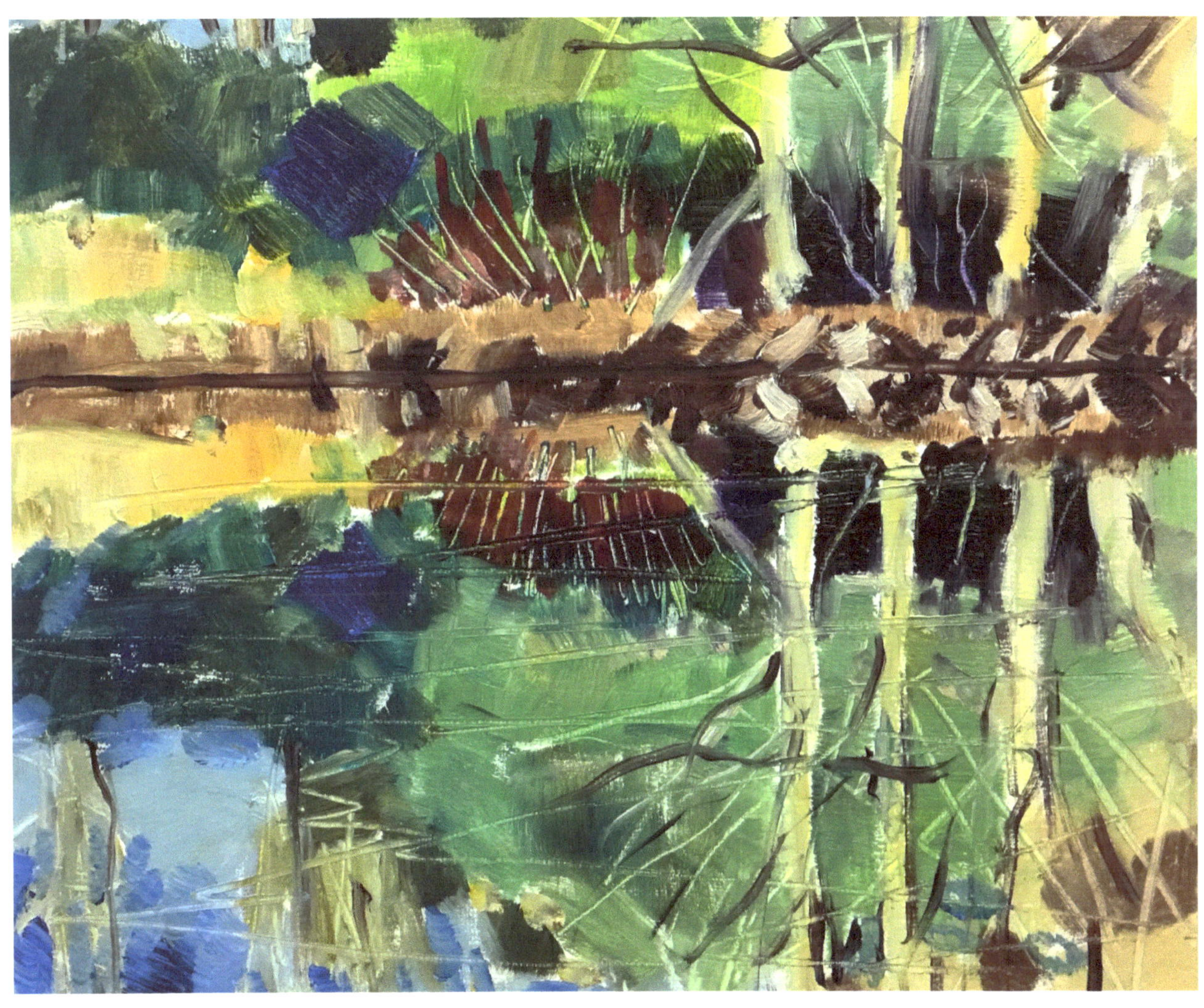

14/01/22
Rosemoor Lake
/// craftsman.latitudes.cellos

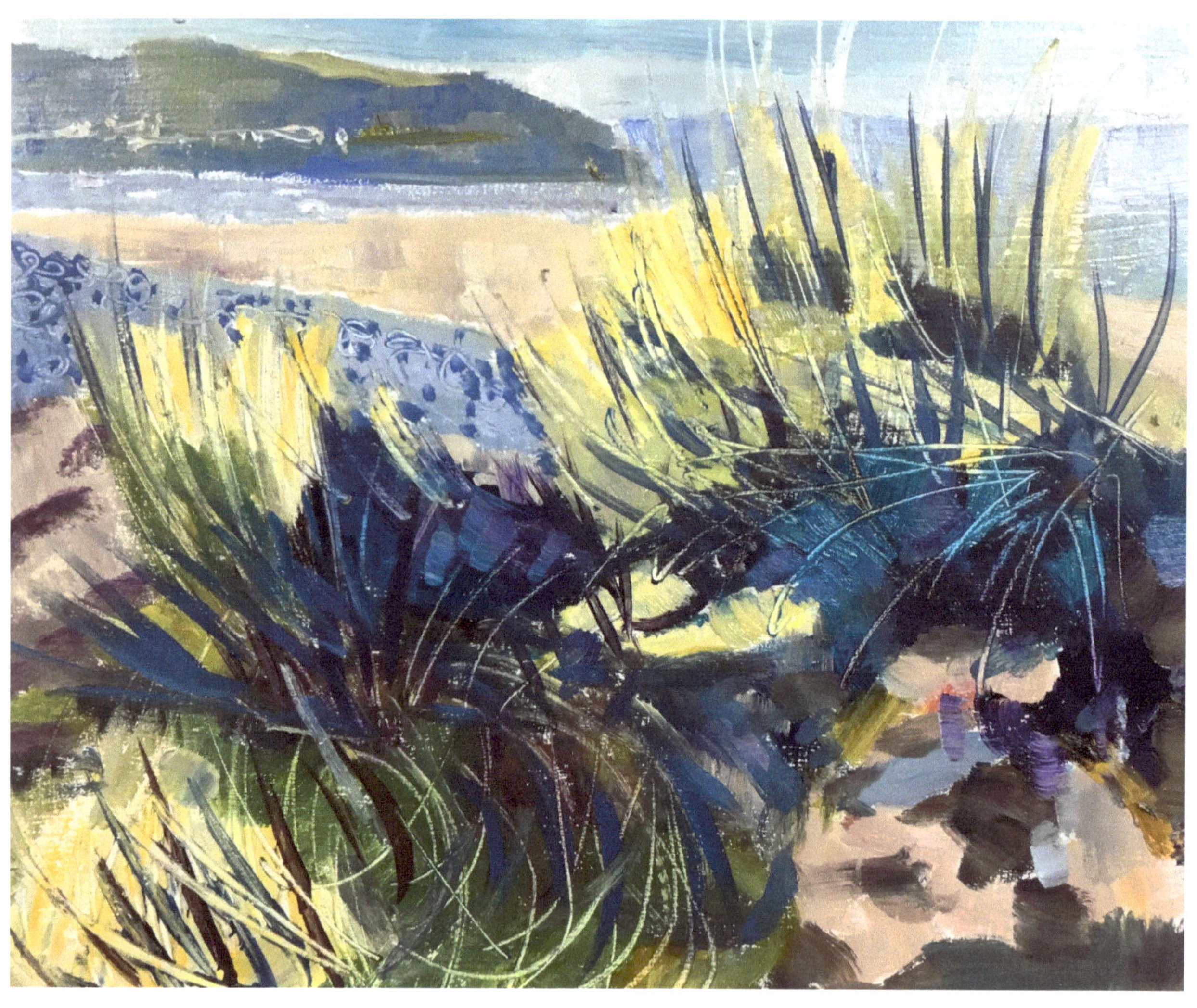

17/01/22
Westward Ho! Beach
/// guesswork.euphoria.staples

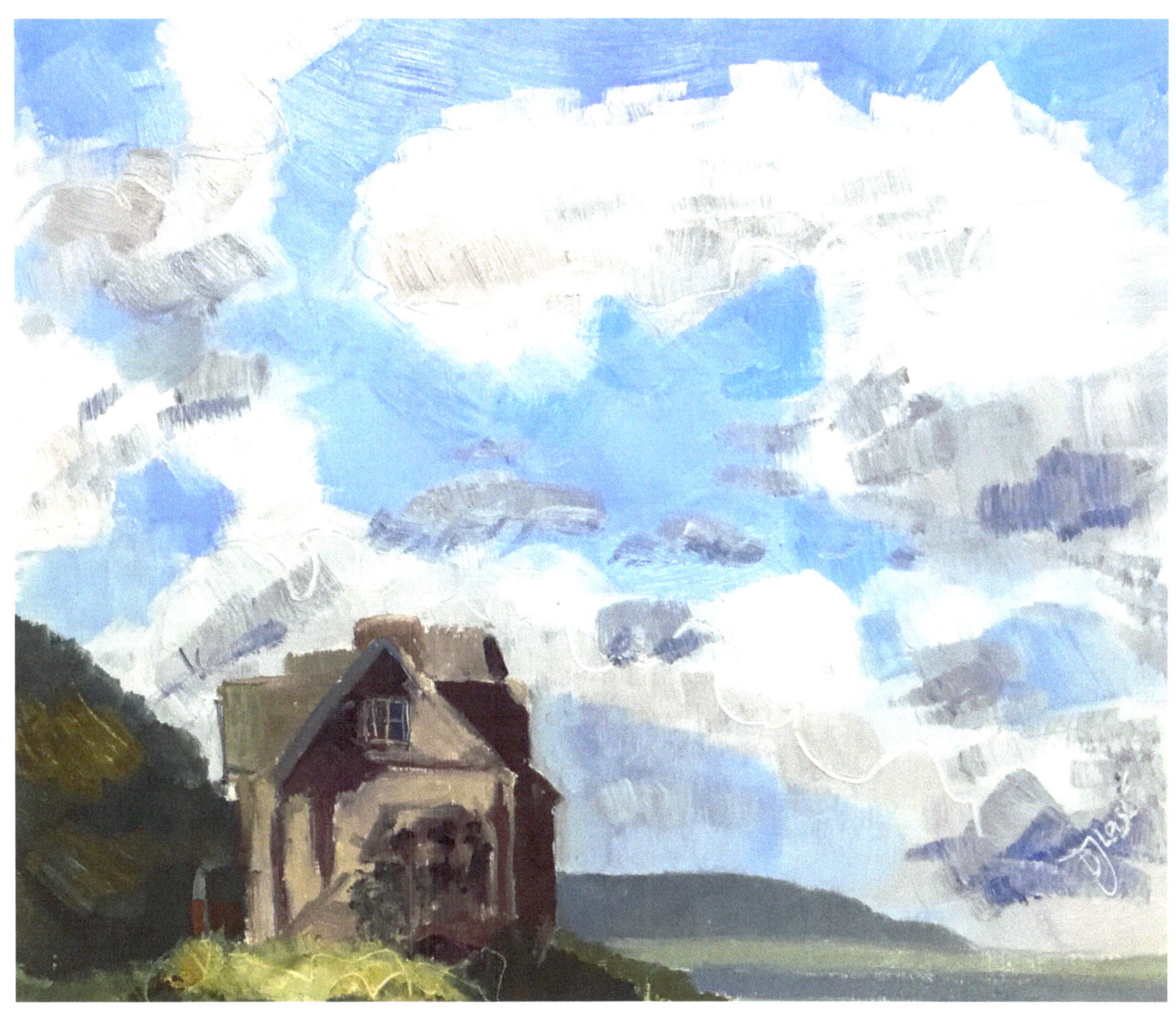

31/01/22
Seagate House from the Pier House
/// alert.prose.swears

February

It was obvious now that I needed to really ensure that the rhythm was accompanied by good practice. This meant making sure I had the right painting out kit. It was still so cold and my layers of overalls, painting coats, hats, gloves, thermals and a huge flask of tea made being outside each day possible. Cleaning everything as soon as I got home ready to go out the day after was so much better than having to do it the next day. It was important that I was filling my pochade boxes with boards, brushes and paint and making sure I was priming the boards well in advance so the gesso had dried for long enough. Each board has been thrice primed in acrylic gesso.

My En Plein Air class were proving to be every bit as brave as I thought they might need to be and were heading out with me into all weathers every Monday morning. Some days it was really tough but somehow exhilarating. I had to be sure I would be OK in the winter as starting in January ensured the project would finish in winter too...

I was really enjoying the structure of the trees in winter and misty light. The beach is full of power at this time of year too which is challenging and brilliant to capture. It's hard to paint when it's windy so I was working out how to do that as well, mostly turning my car boot away from the wind and painting from sitting in there or finding a building to hide behind!

22/02/22
Instow beach
/// stared.adding.rigs

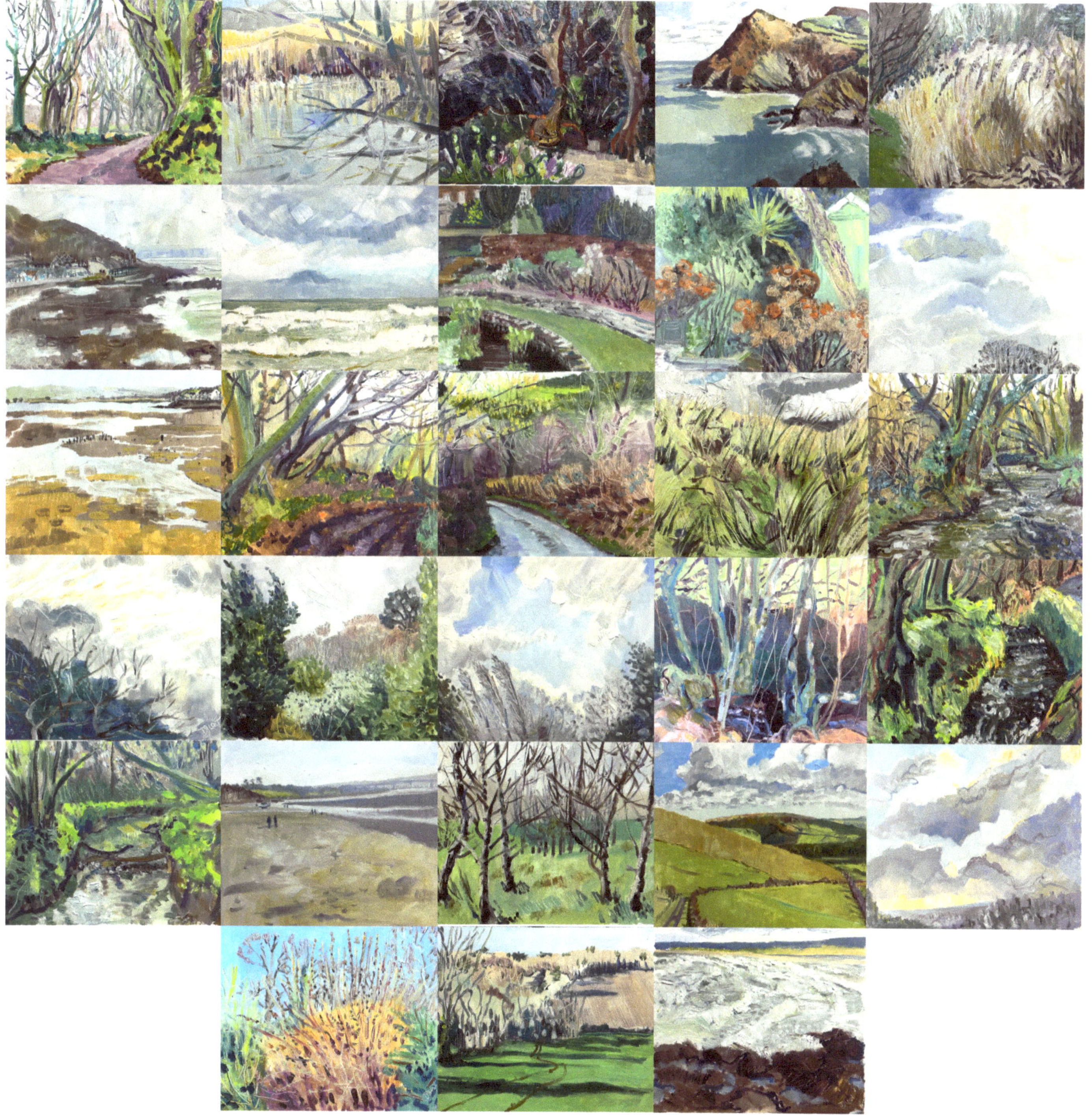

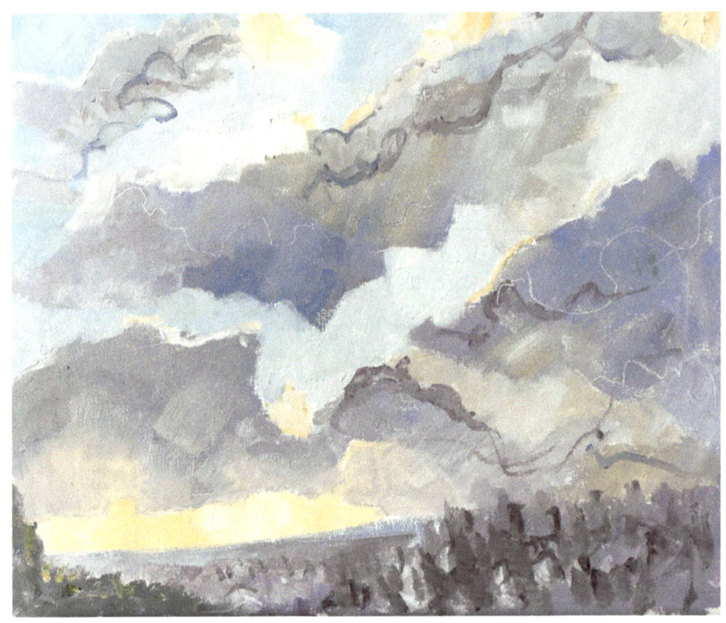

25/02/22
Sunrise over Bideford
///banks.slower.number

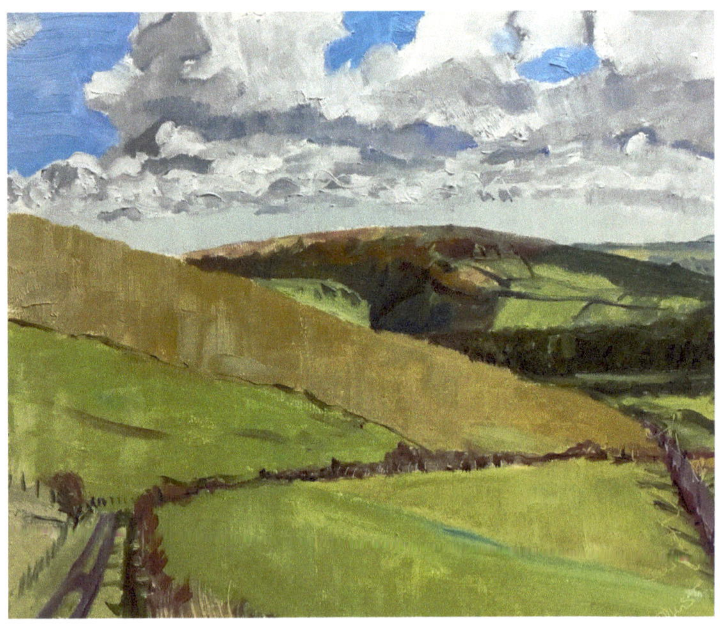

24/02/22
Hangley Cleave & Long Holcombe
/// traded.parked.intelligible

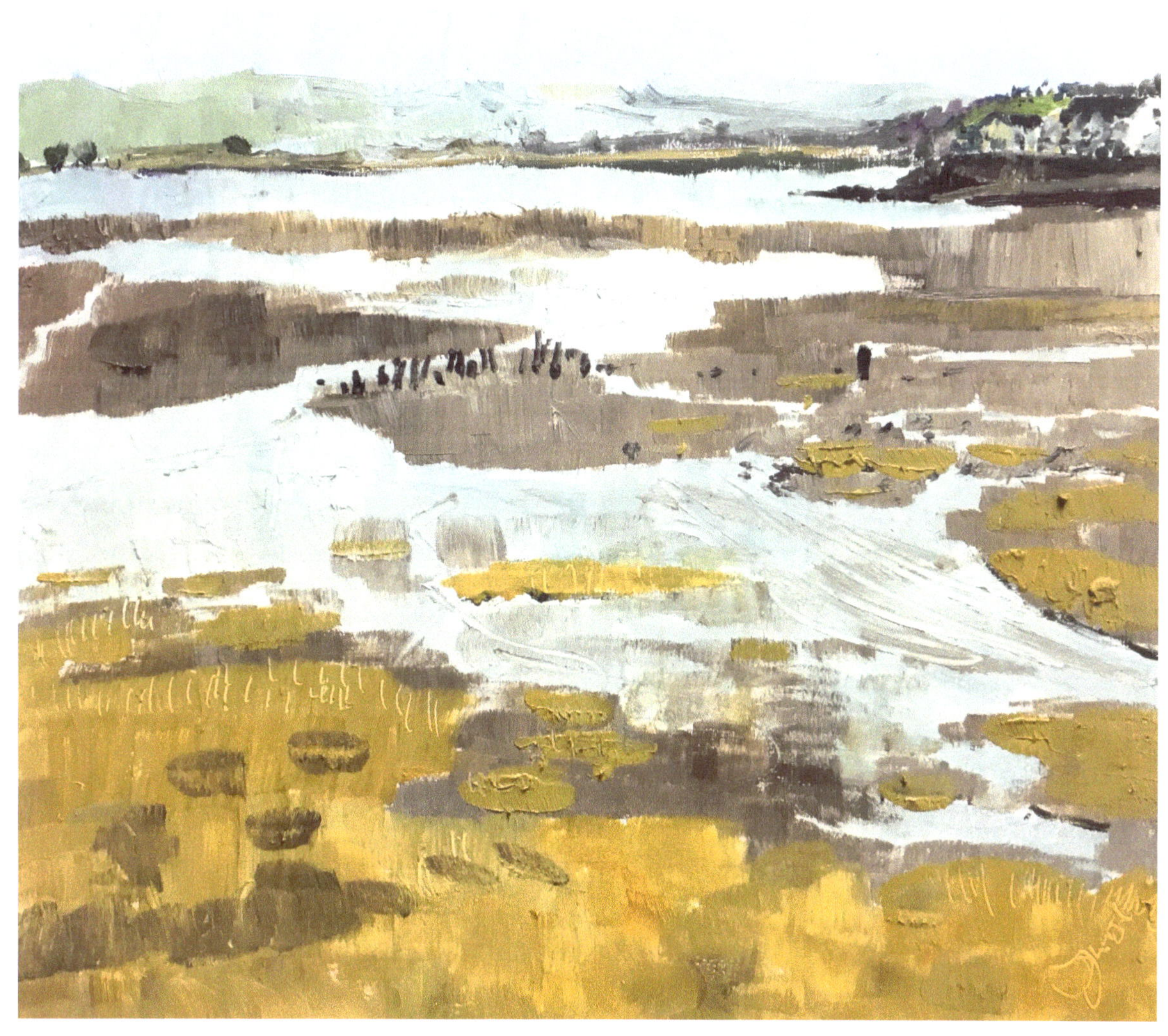

11/02/22
Northam Burrows, Skern
/// surfers.root.intentions

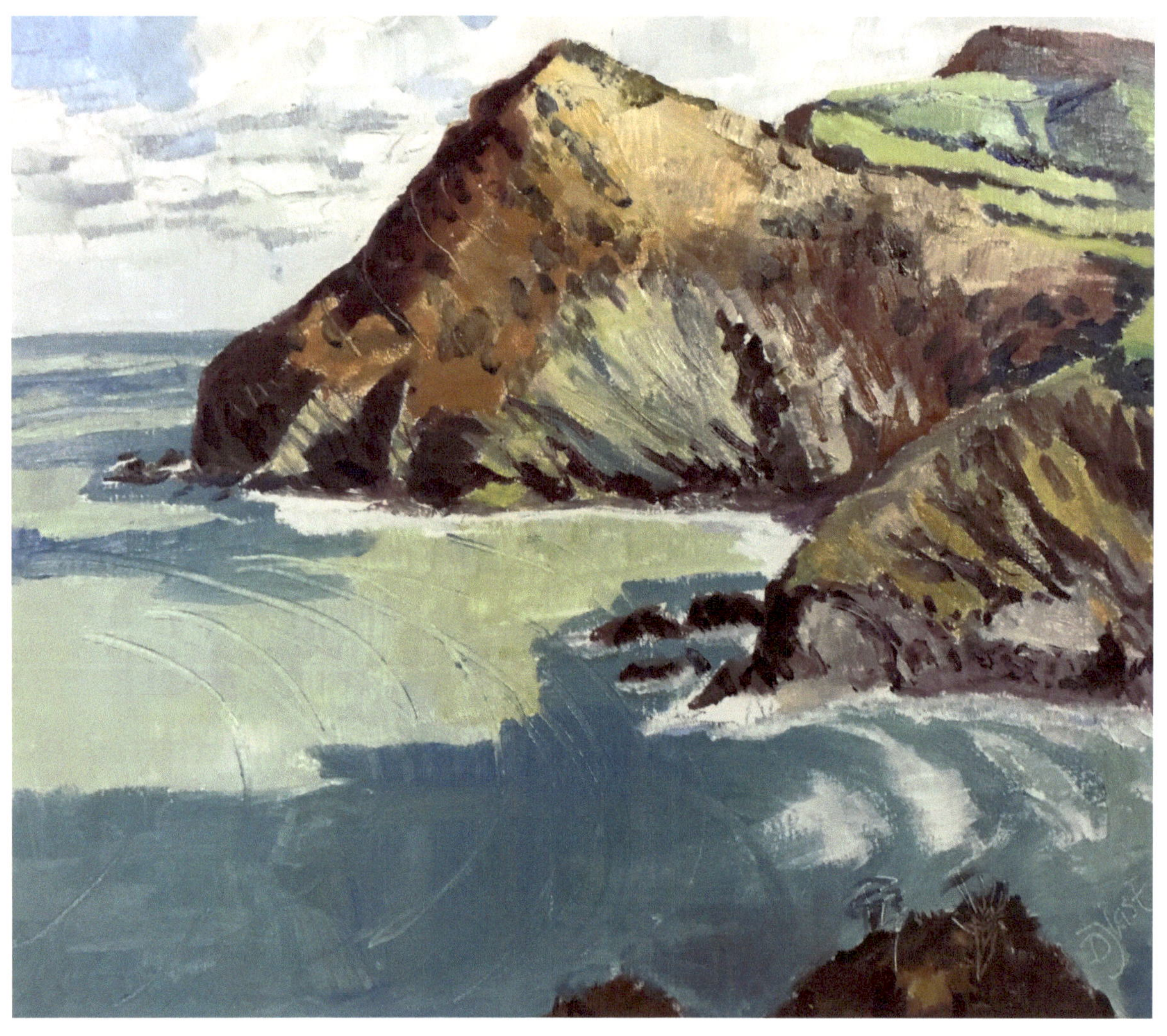

04/02/22
Sandy Cove
/// poodle.manuals.relievess

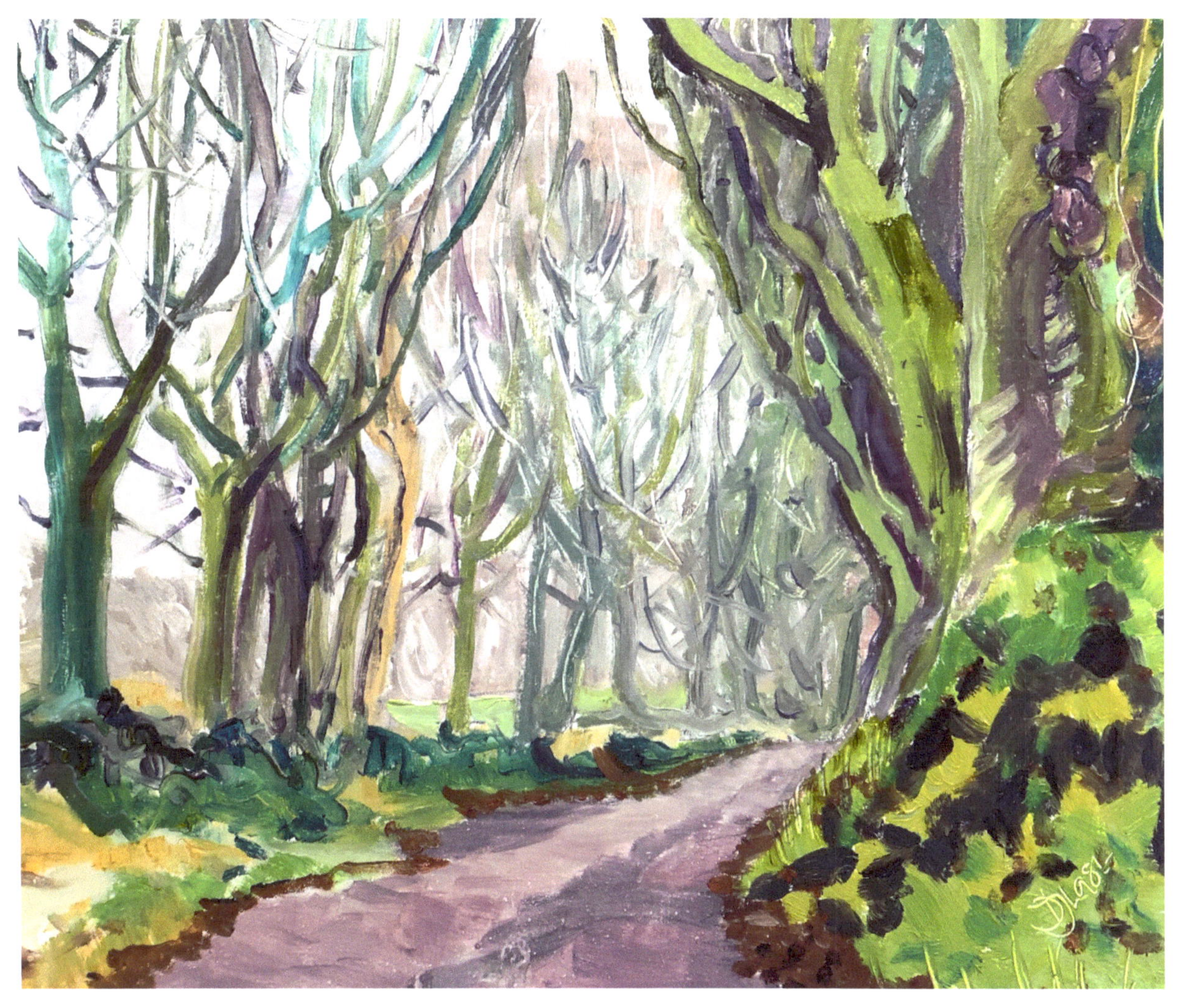

01/02/22
Bridestow Tree Tunnel
/// busted.ballparks.tenderss

March

The hints of spring were there and some days it was warmer to paint out than it had been. Little flashes of yellow and the warming colour in the tree branches appeared as they thickened and began to bud. I enjoyed adding fresher, brighter colours and though at the start of the month there were still the brown-greys of winter in the trees, as the month neared the end the lime-greens of spring were being well established in the hedgerows. At RHS Rosemoor there were wonderful colours to be found, especially in the Stone Garden with its abundant magnolias.

01/03/22
From the Boathouse, Instow
/// lifetimes.whoever.commuting

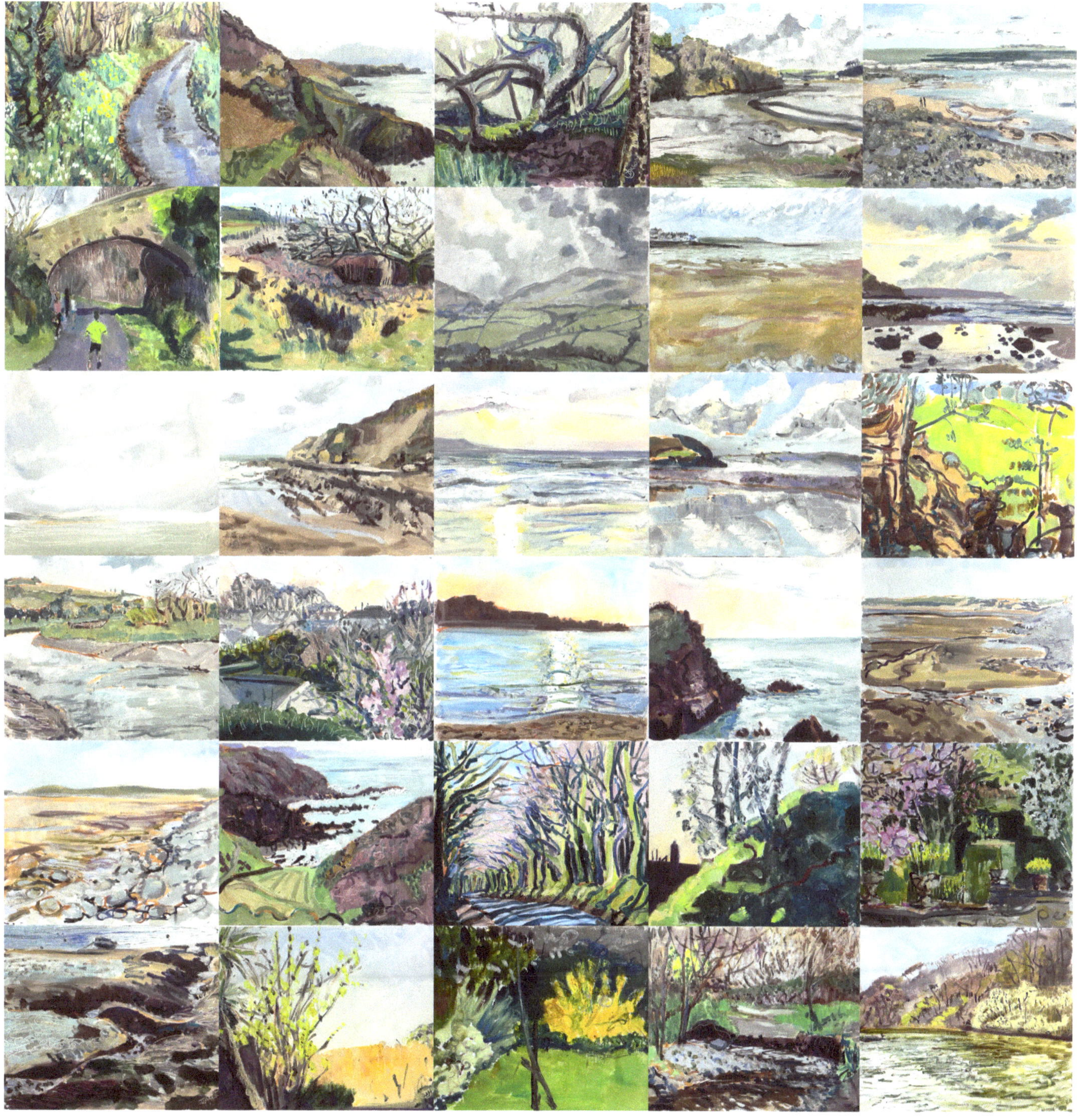

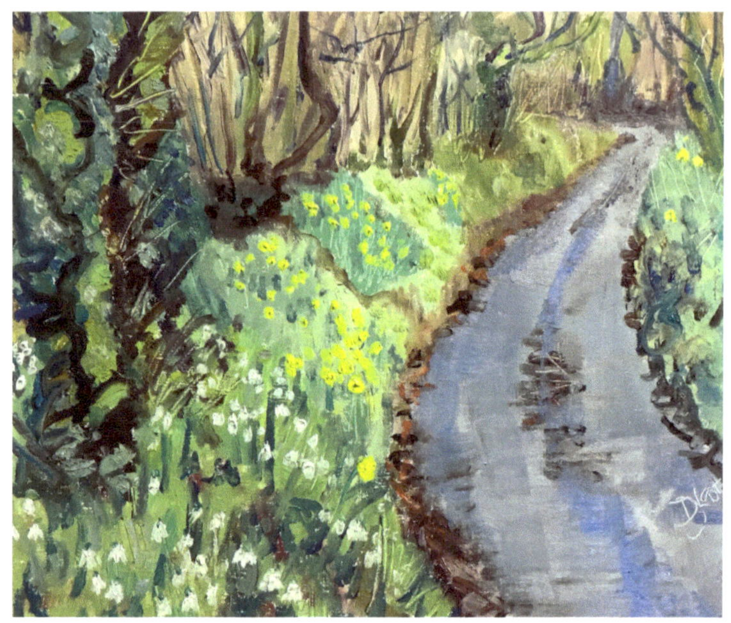

01/03/22
Devon Lane, Woodsley Mill
/// factoring.ready.modifiers

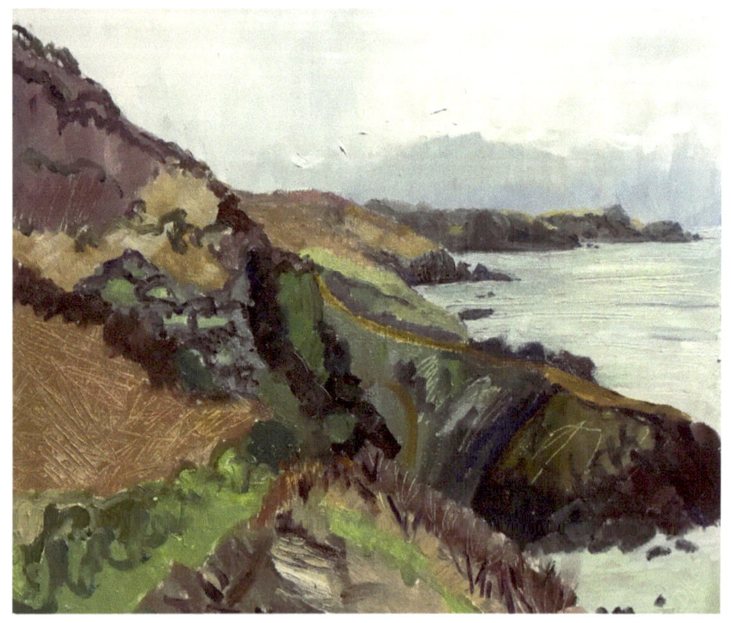

02/03/22
The Torrs, Ilfracombe
/// spend.tinned.afternoon

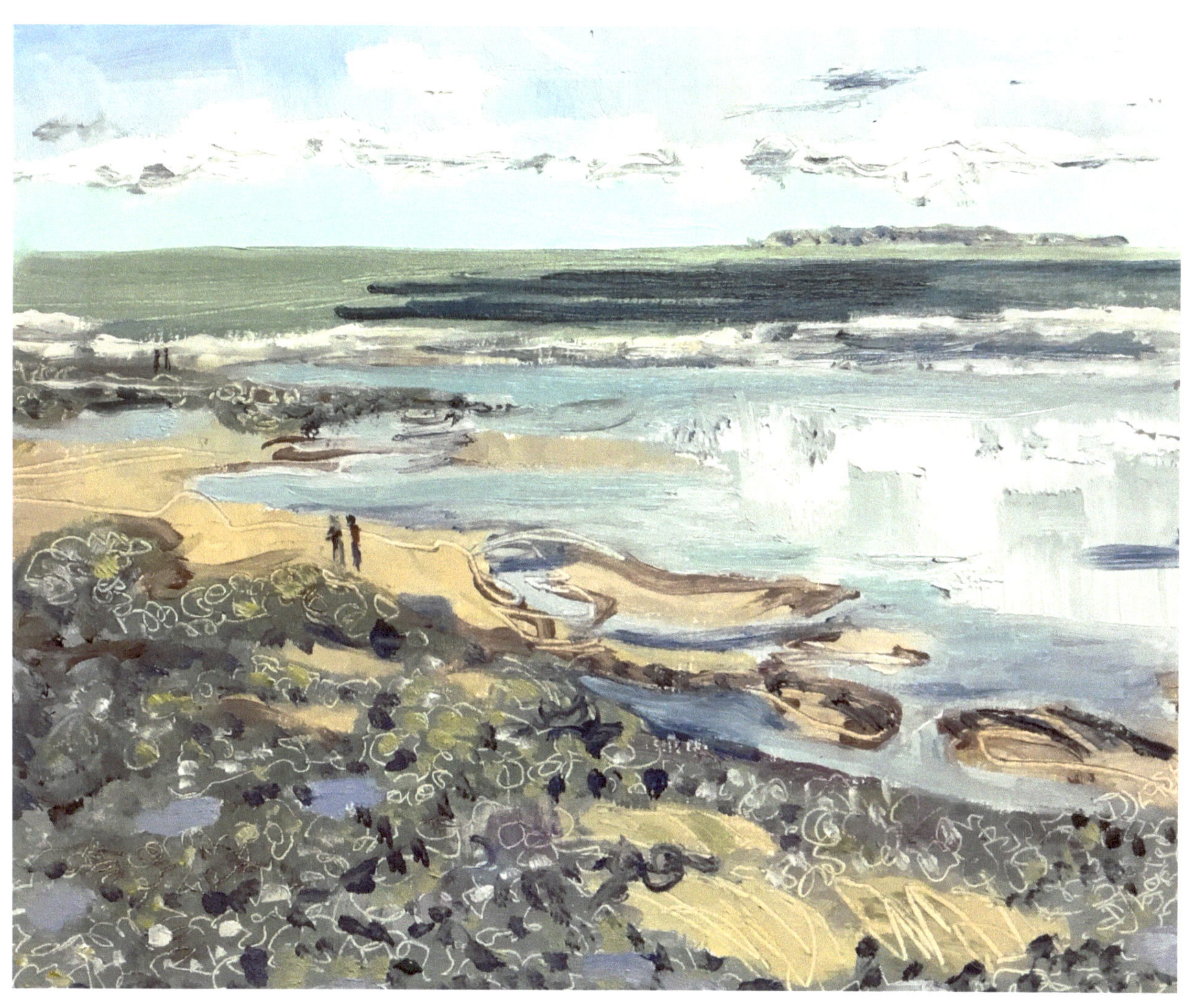

05/03/22
Westward Ho! to Lundy
prickly.engrossed.clap

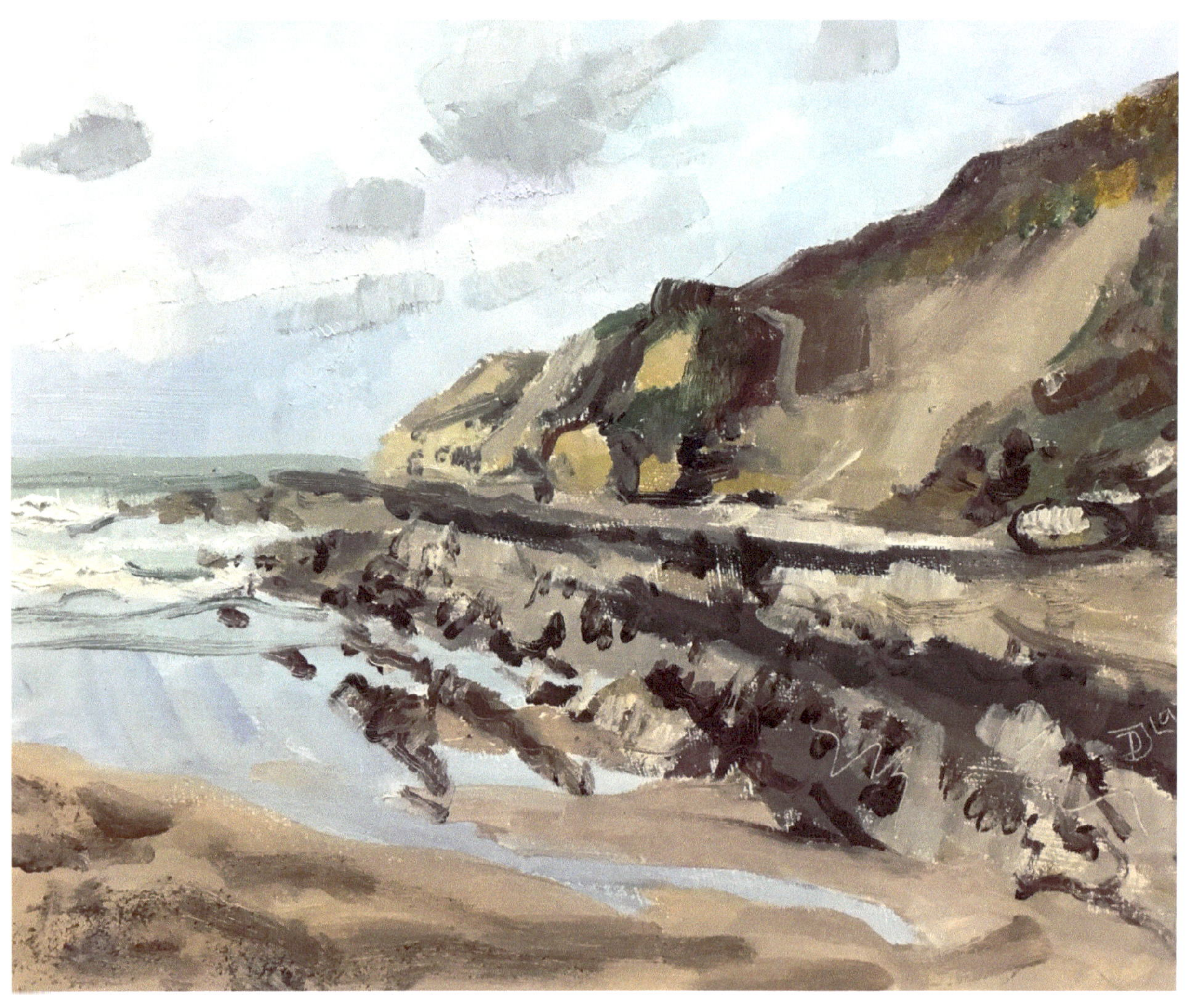

12/03/22
Saunton Sands
/// brother.sneezing.daunting

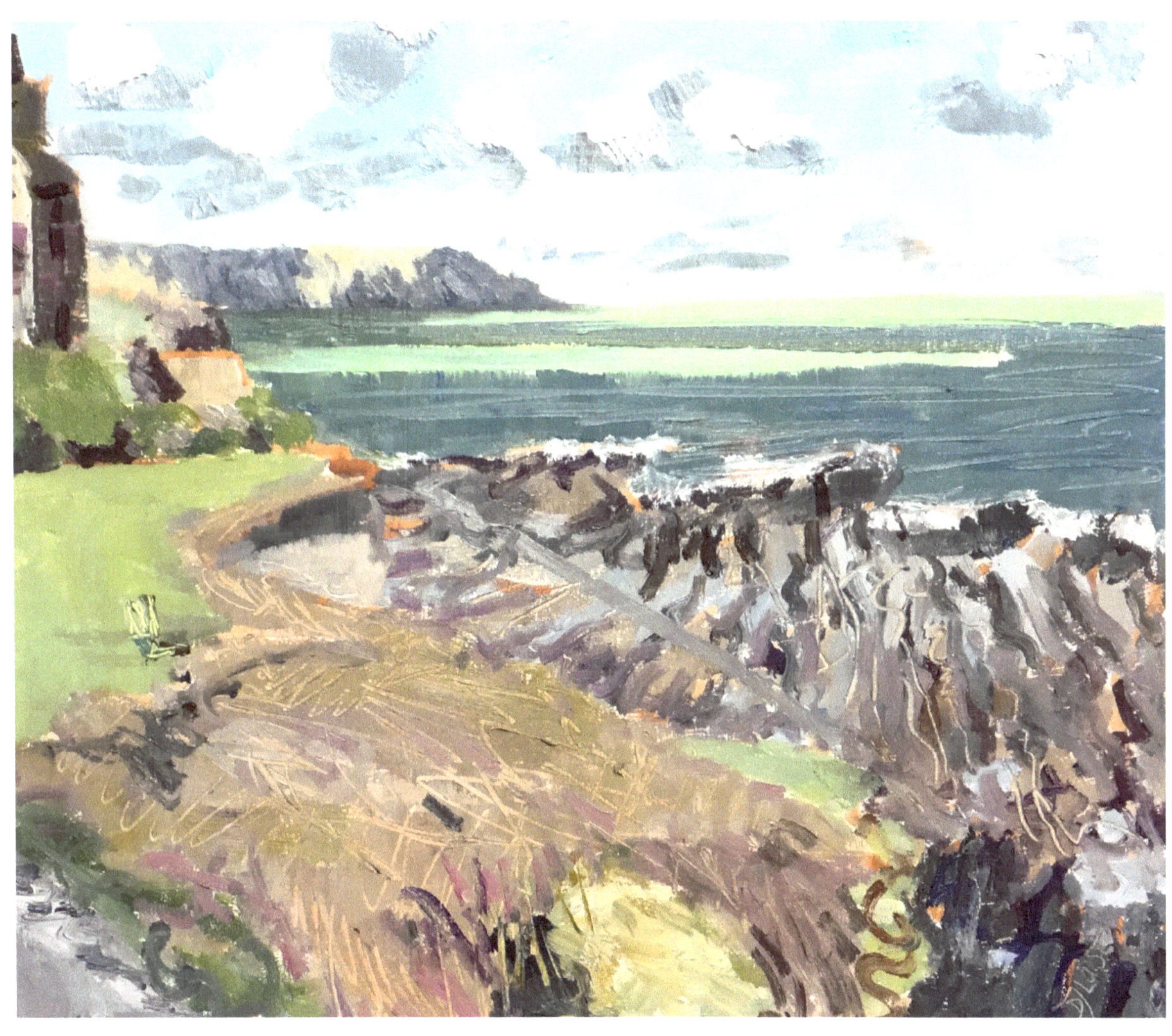

31/03/22
From the Pierhouse
/// deny.yards.mill

April

This month I had to work out a bit more fully how to travel with my paints and how to fit it into a busier schedule. Our daughter Chloe was getting married in May and I started the month of April with a hen do in Kent. On the journey down I came off the A303 and headed to Stourhead and painted throughout the hen weekend. Painting at various points in the day there was a bit of me that didn't want to separate myself off to paint and I chose a less interesting location that had a good sky so I could stay with everyone sitting outside in the unseasonably warm sun. It hinted at how it might feel to paint on the wedding day. I enjoyed being warmer and the colour that was pouring into the landscape. I began painting with a lot more lemon yellow and brighter colours.

04/04/22
View from the Boathouse
/// madness.contracting.pose

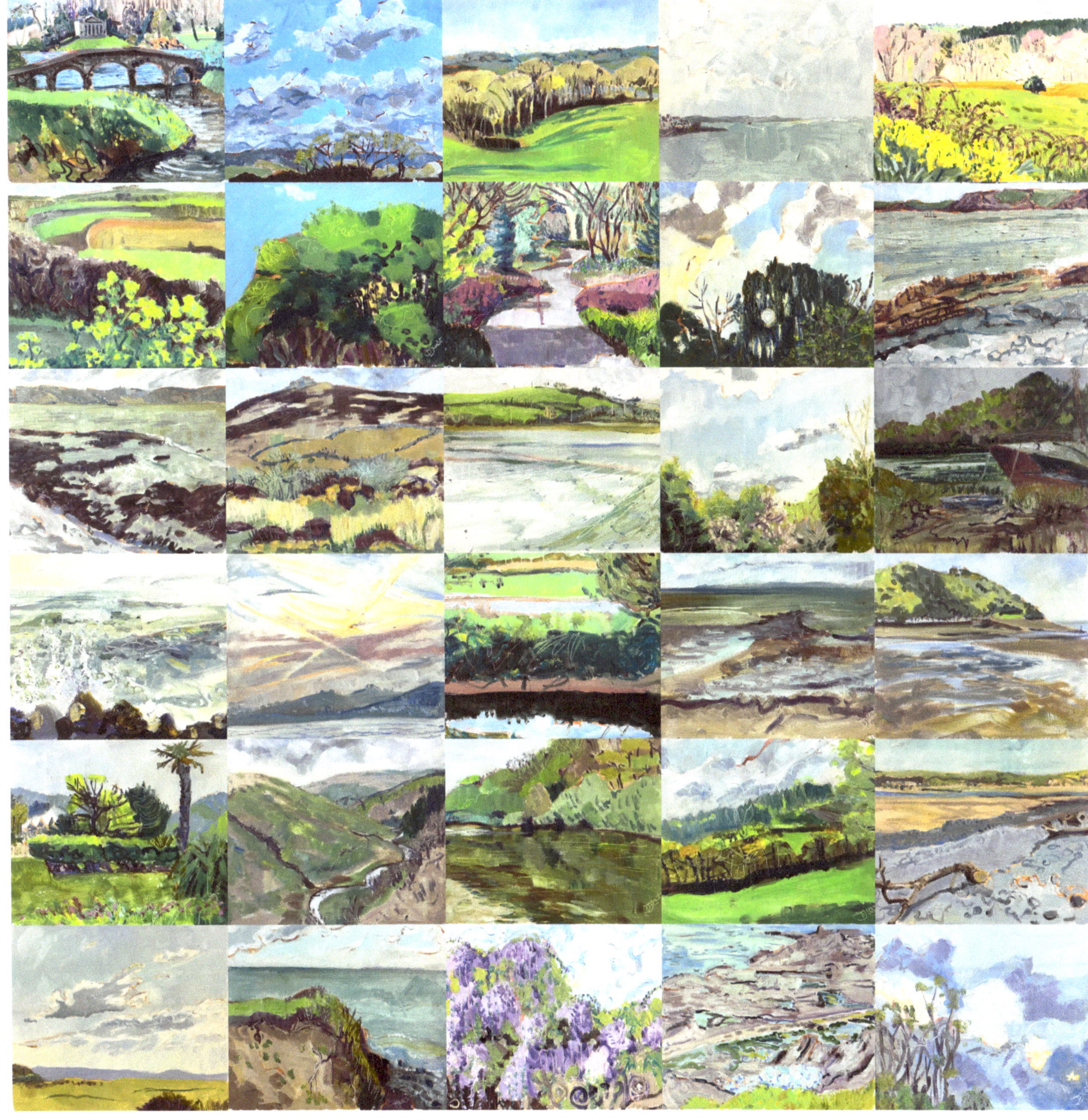

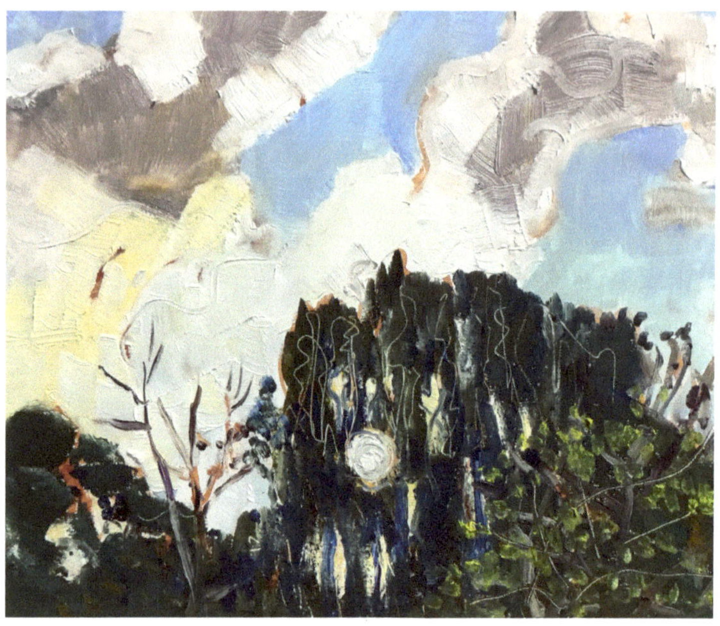

09/04/22
Morning Light Through Trees
/// void.cones.number

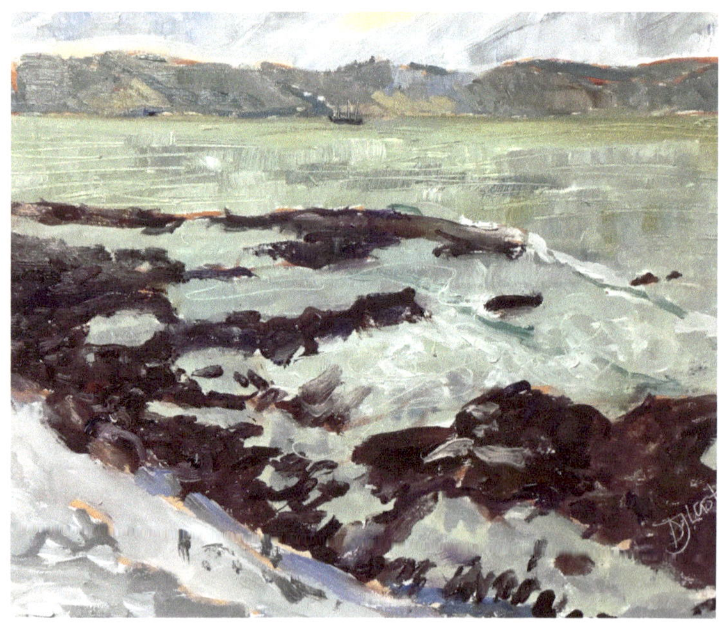

11/04/22
Greencliff Beach
/// remotes.bypasses.dopes

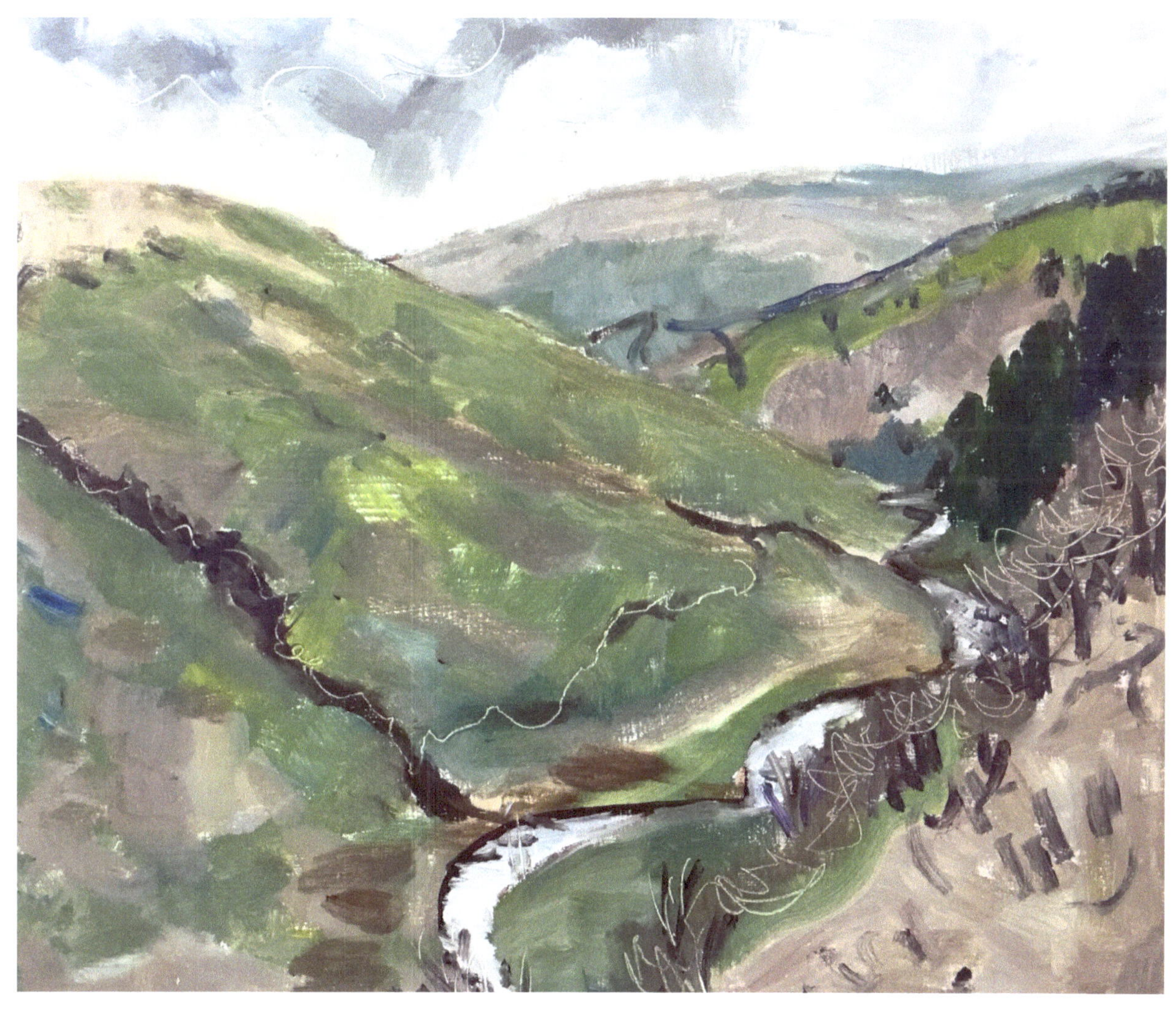

22/04/22
Road to Simonsbath
/// stops.prepped.staples

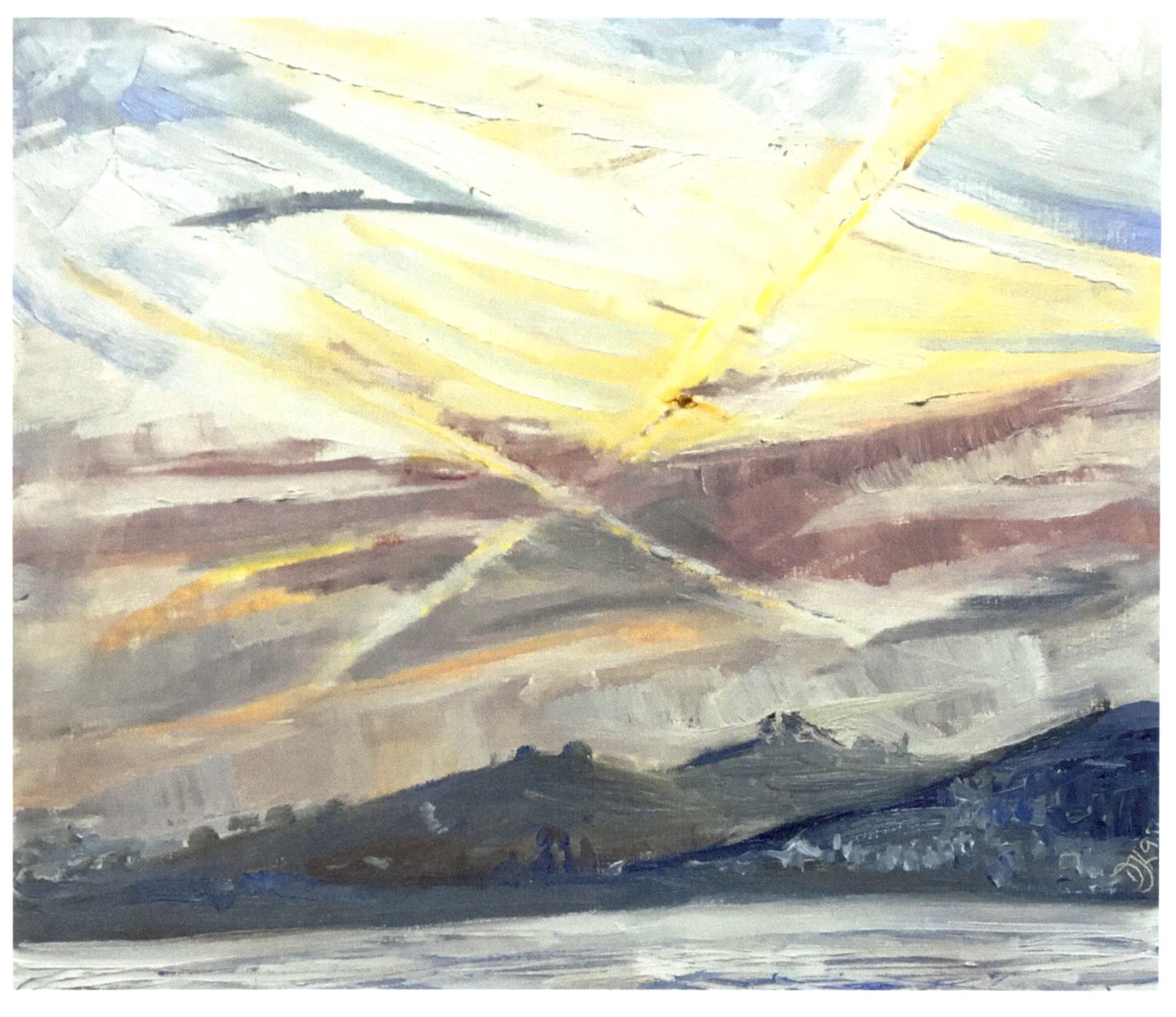

17/04/22
Easter Day, Sunrise
/// overnight.constrain.smooth

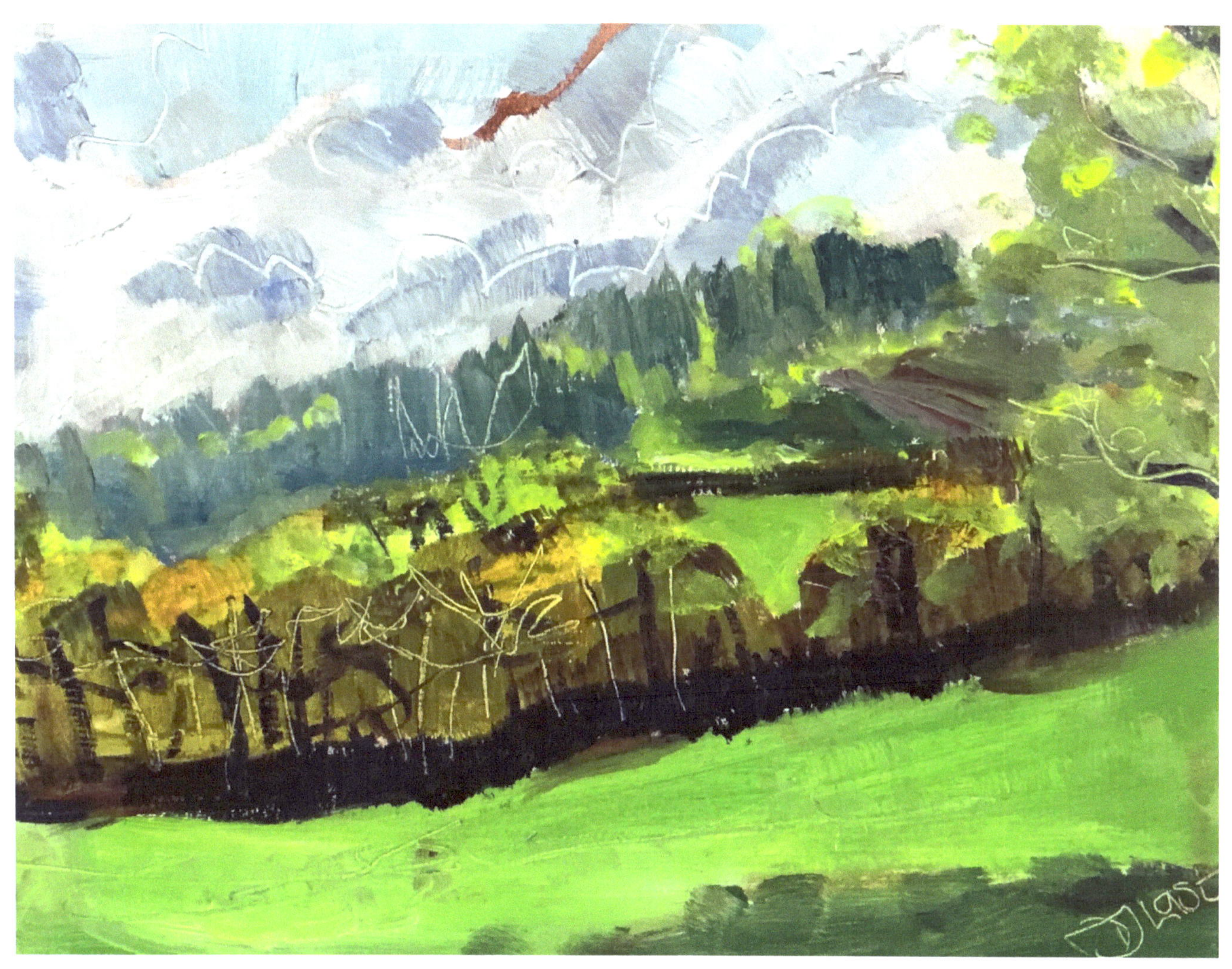

24/04/22
Drive Home Through Parkham
/// drive.magnum.panoramic

May

Suddenly there are pinks and whites bursting into the landscape, cascading into the garden at Orleigh Court as I painted the amazing rhododendrons. The spring colours were bursting into the trees and foliage everywhere, with blossom on the side of roads and even in the middle of roundabouts. I had to be careful about how I captured this without getting a bit overwhelmed and too cliched. Some days I headed to the sea where things were a little easier to describe and had become strongly familiar if still ever changing. This month there were lots of events and travel. Most importantly we travelled to Kent for the wedding and although people are amazed that I painted on the wedding day, the days around the wedding were much harder to paint on somehow as we were busy. On the day of the wedding Ross and Chloe had beautiful weather and we were all together with nothing else to do but celebrate. Getting the paints out was easy really as people came and chatted and moved around the garden before the wedding breakfast. This was however the only painting of the entire collection that I did finish off in the studio as I added the bride and groom into it later.

14/05/22
Evening Sun
/// tens.quiet.famous

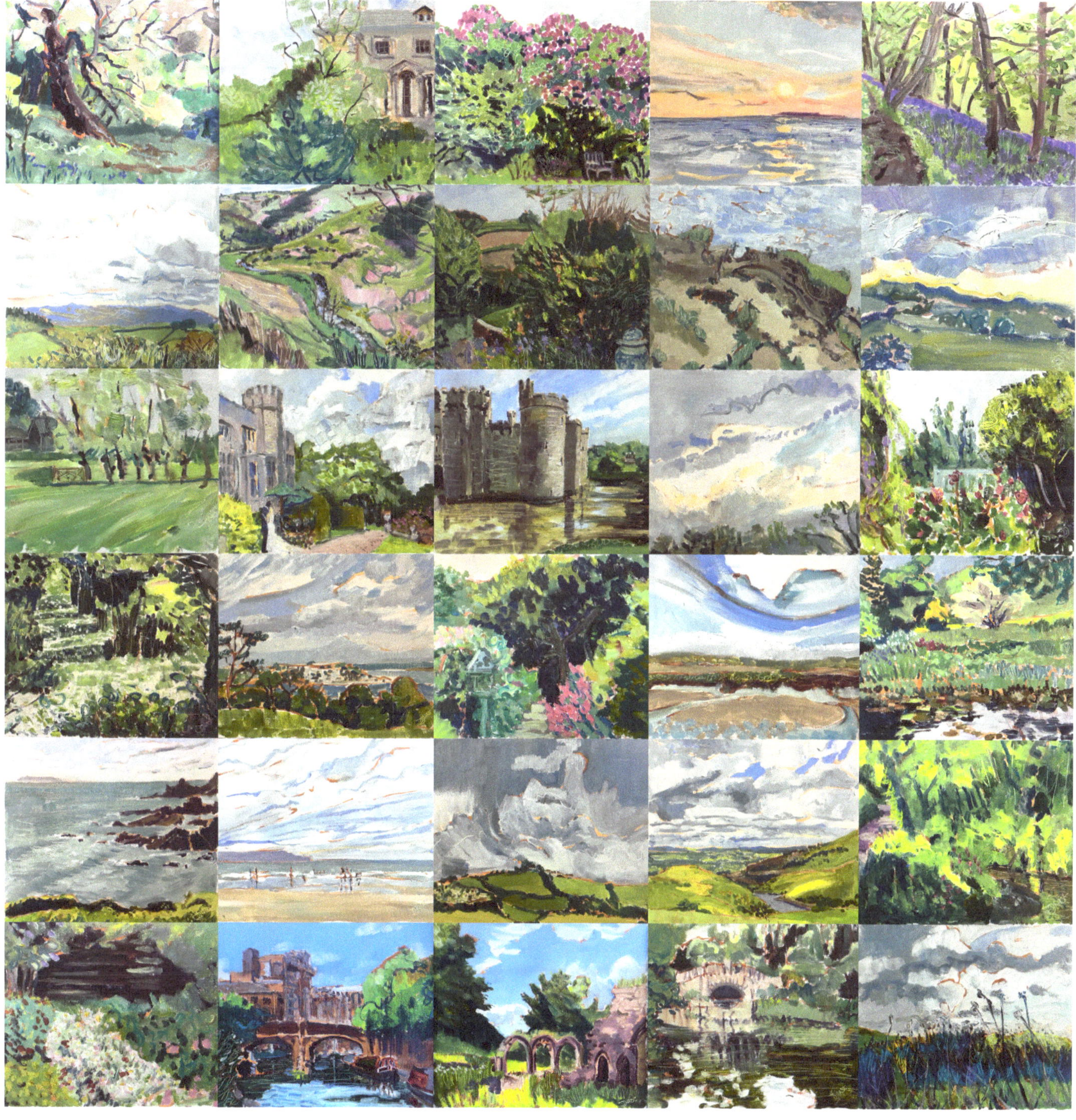

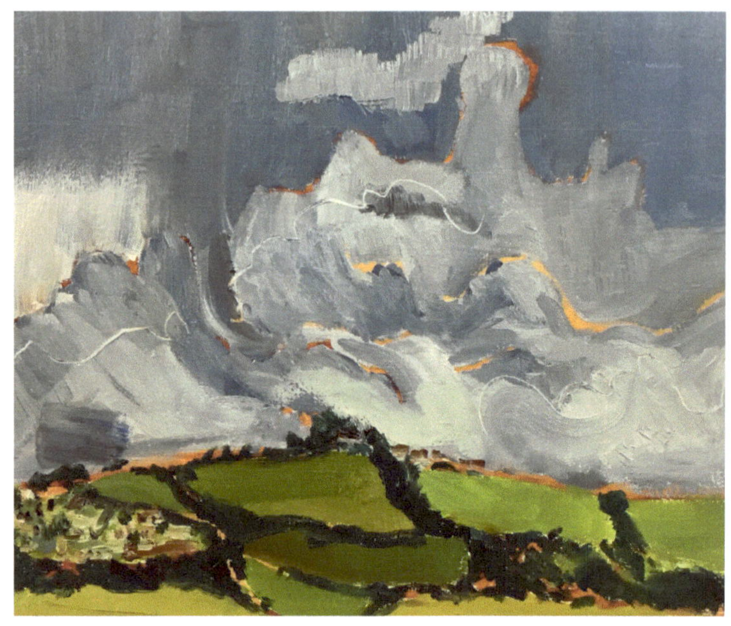

23/05/22
Northam Burrows to Appledore
/// abandons.beaten.towers

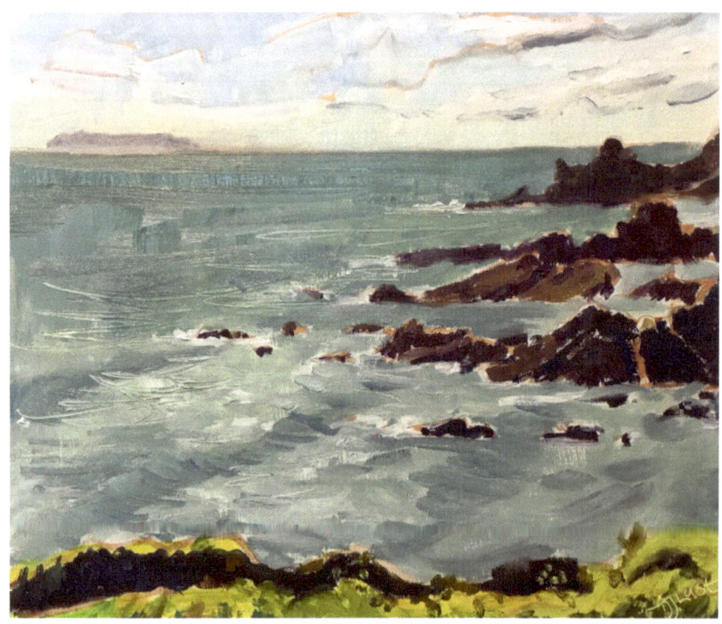

21/05/22
Hartland Quay
/// pushed.producing.wonderfully

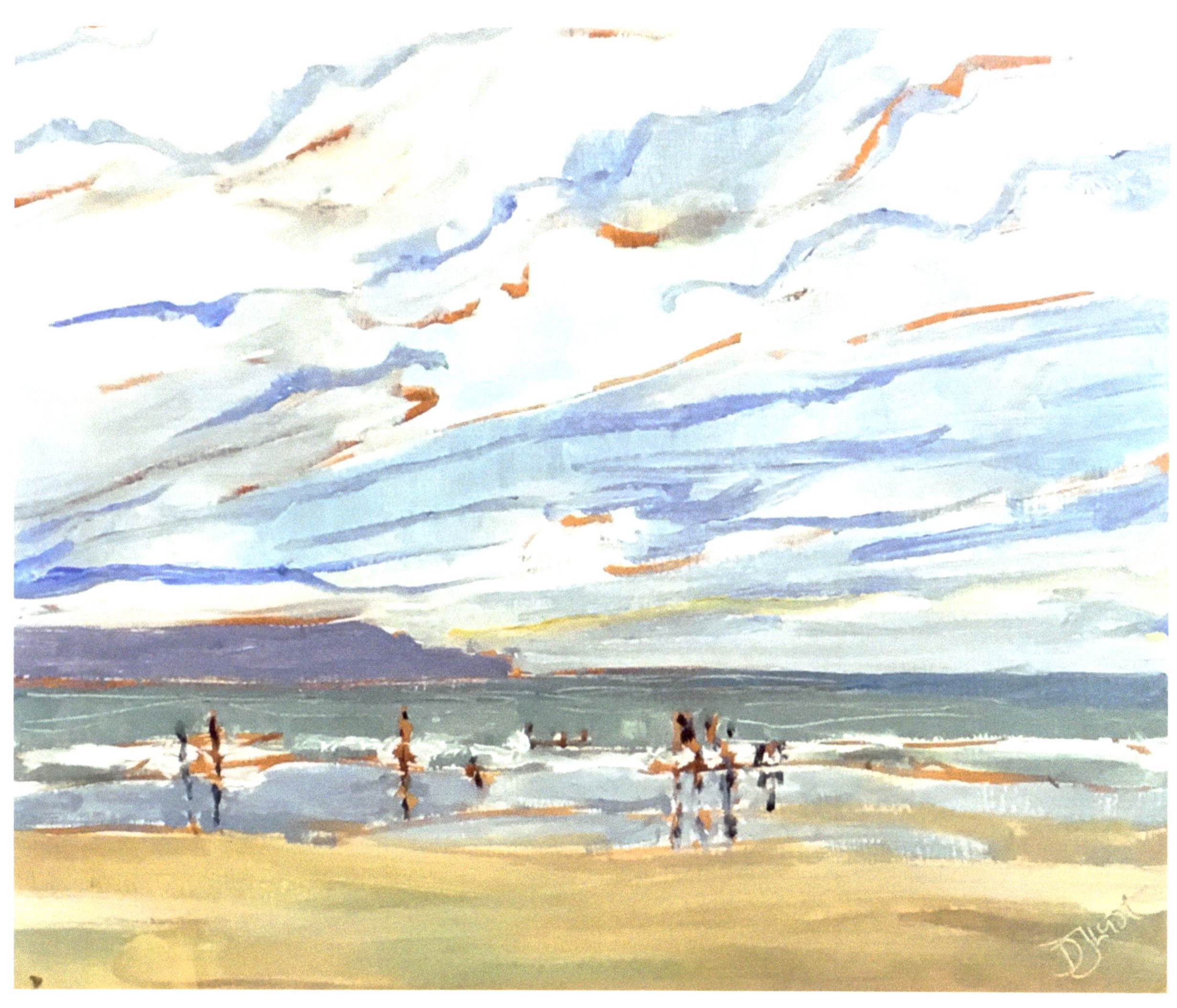

22/05/22
Westward Ho! Beach
/// overlaps.hours. rotation

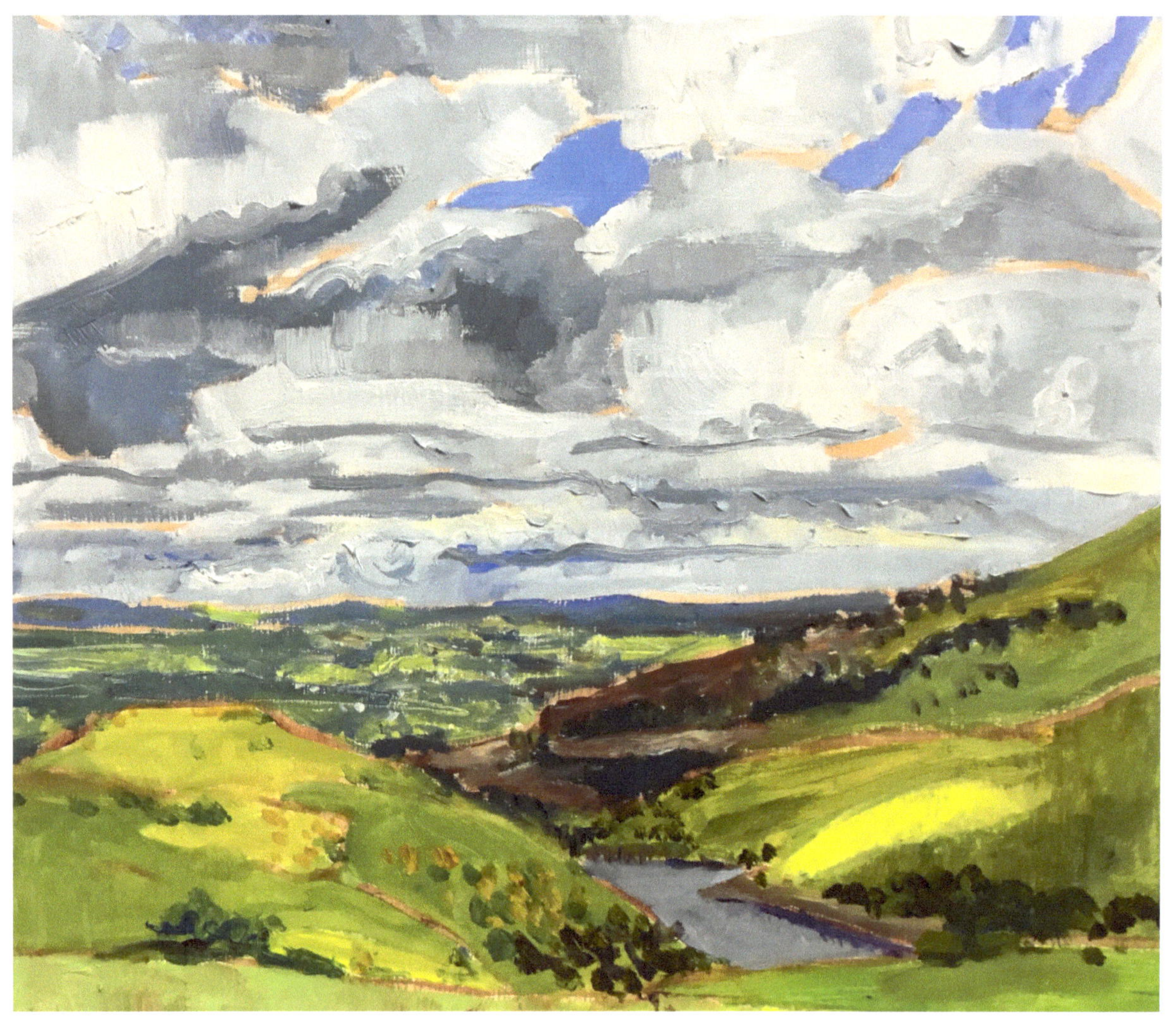

24/05/22
From Sourton Tors
/// bravery.window.increased

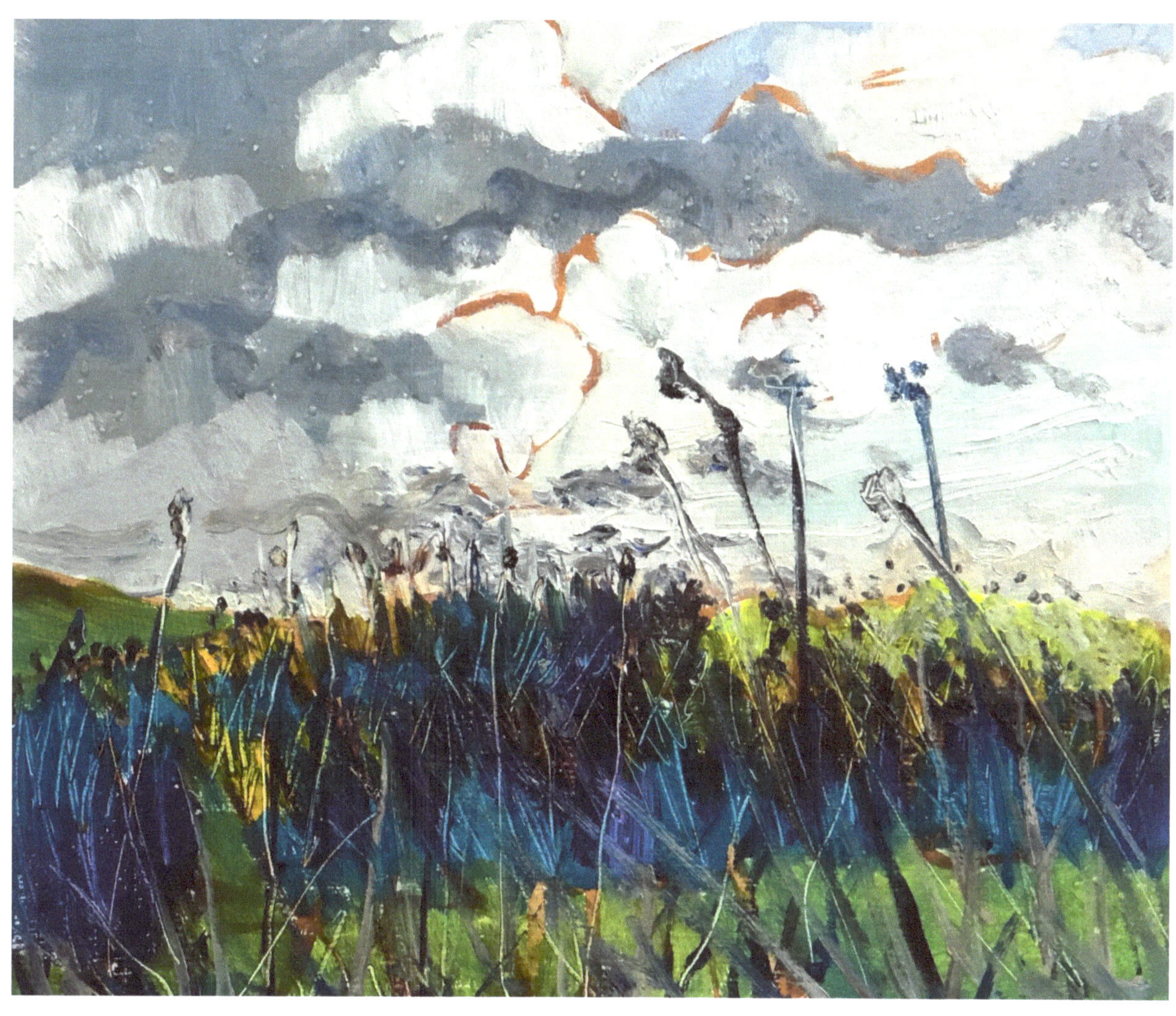

30/05/22
Northam Burrows
/// swear.bends.paddock

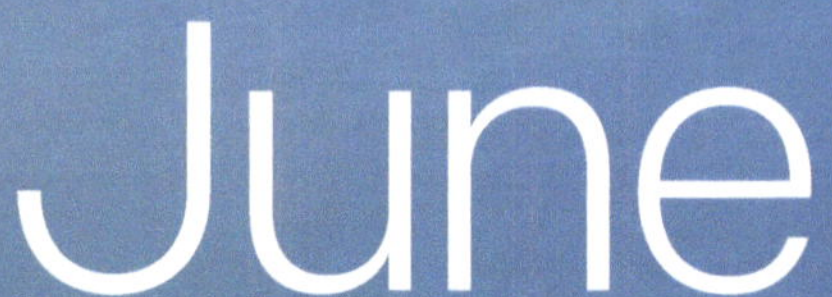

June

There was lots of colour to be enjoyed in June but also a lot of green and it meant I had to find ways to get round that. Sunlit days are perfect for that as there are great shadows and my brilliant location in North Devon meant I had coastline and beaches in glorious abundance. I had lots of dramatic skies to paint as June gave a good mix of weather with wonderful summer clouds and azure blue-sky days. On one day I did just paint the blue sky and I actually had to spend quite a bit of time colour matching. I also enjoyed the opportunity to paint Devon valleys with the hazy light of summer giving a wonderful sense of the distance across the landscape.

I introduced a purple into some of the landscapes with varying degrees of success. It was good to adjust the palette I was using as it mixed things up. The purple was a great foil to the greens of summer and gave beautiful shadows. It felt good to get to the end of June as it was halfway through. It was amazing exploring beautiful North Devon and heading up and down lanes and moors I might have not have gone to without the project as a nudge to do so.

06/06/22
Westward Ho! Beach
/// lively.tried.strictest

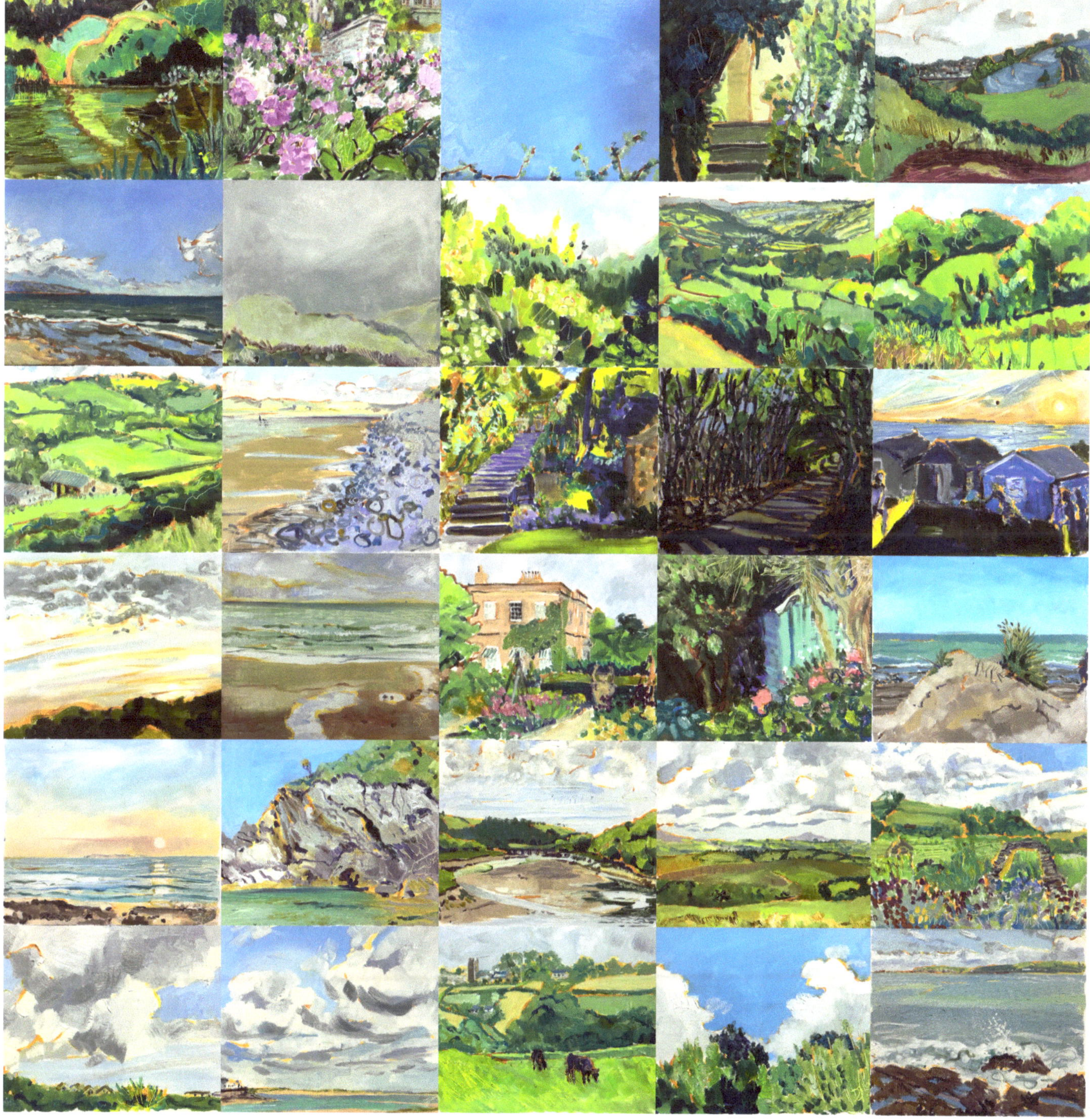

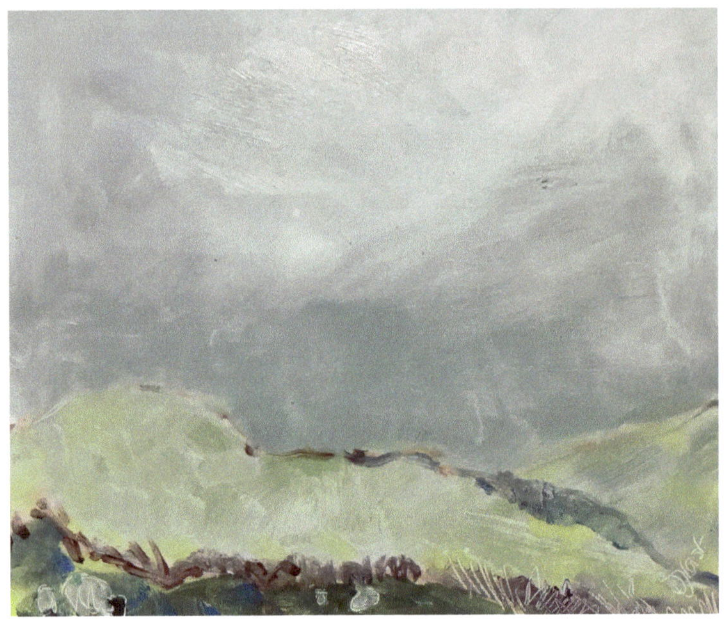

07/06/22
Dartmoor in Summer Mist
/// protests.slumped.optimists

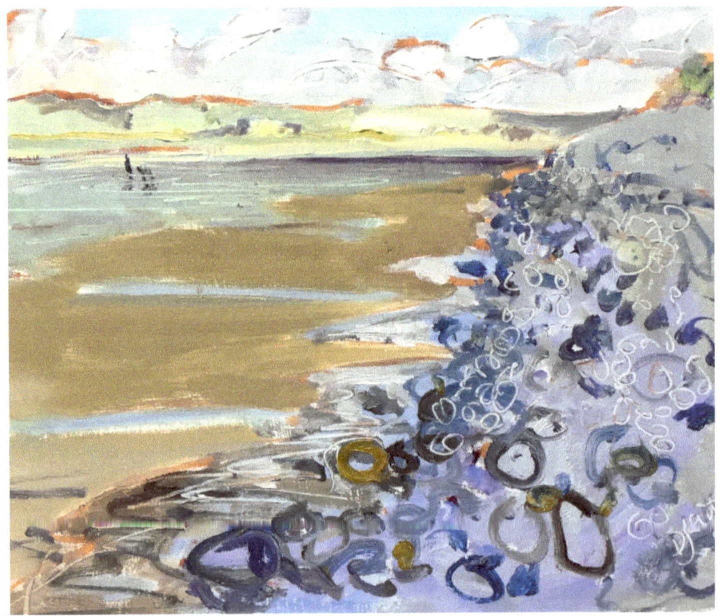

12/06/22
Westward Ho! Ridge
/// listed.ooze.baseline

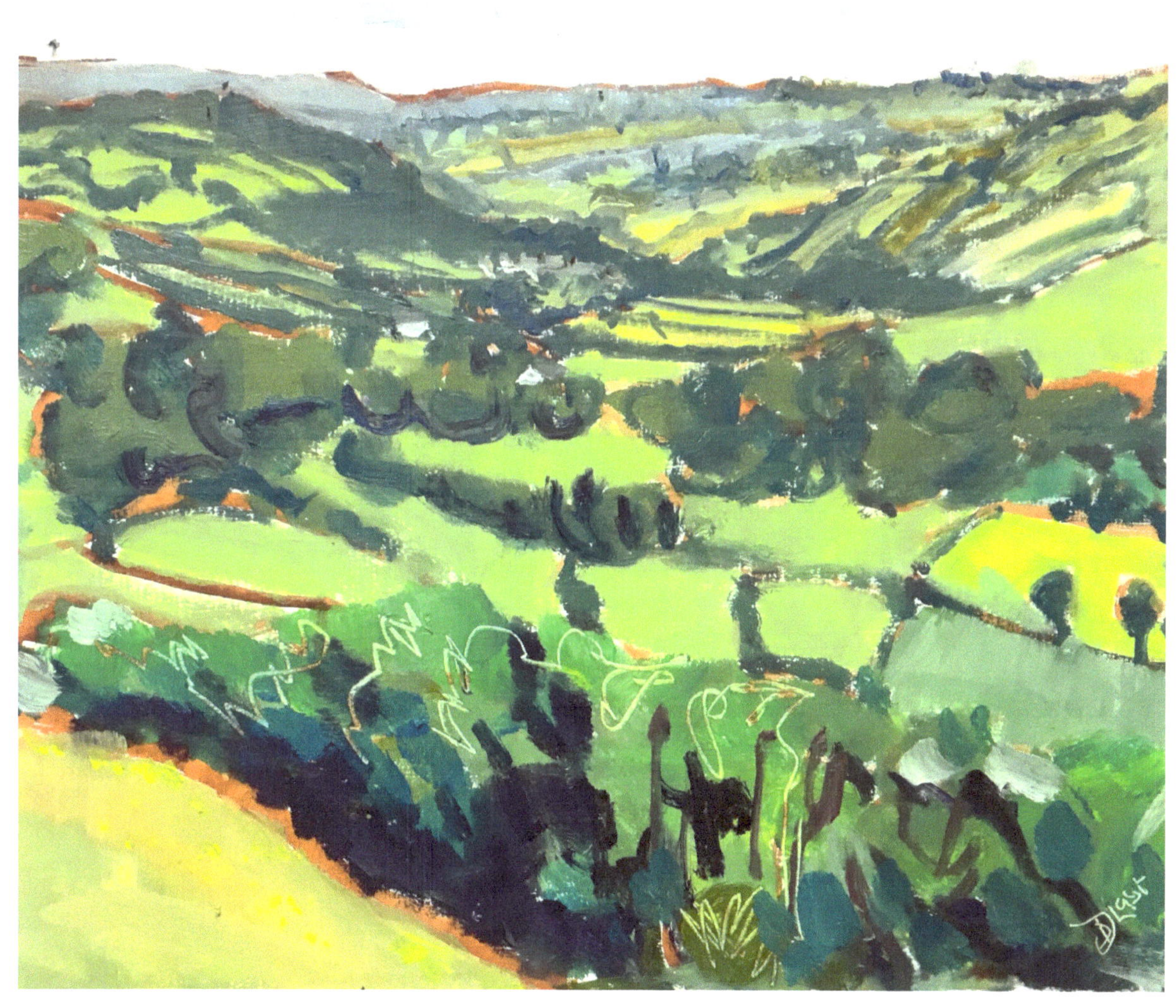

09/06/22
Dumpton Hill
/// video.points.grape

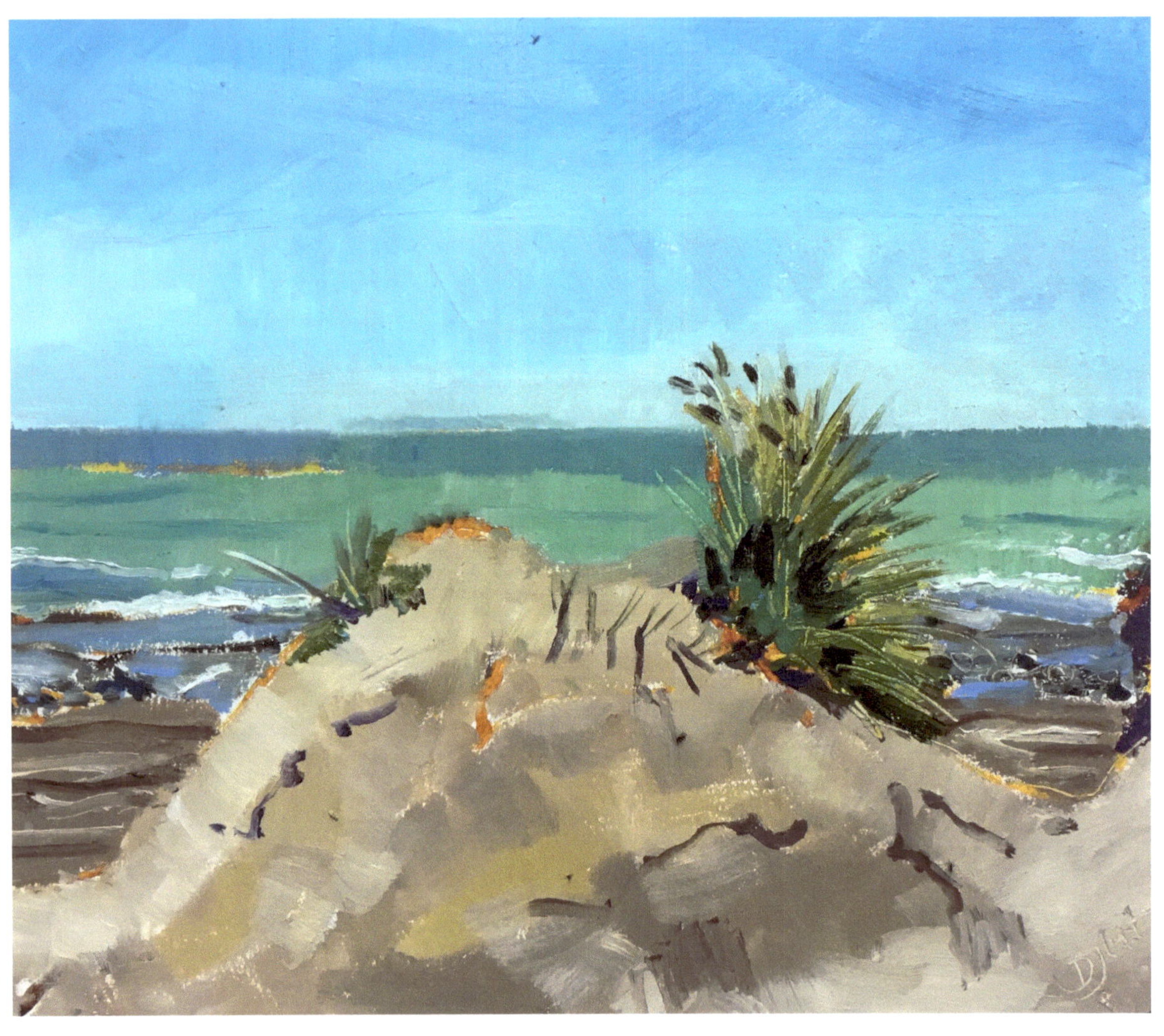

20/06/22
Sand Dune
/// protest.cascade.camps

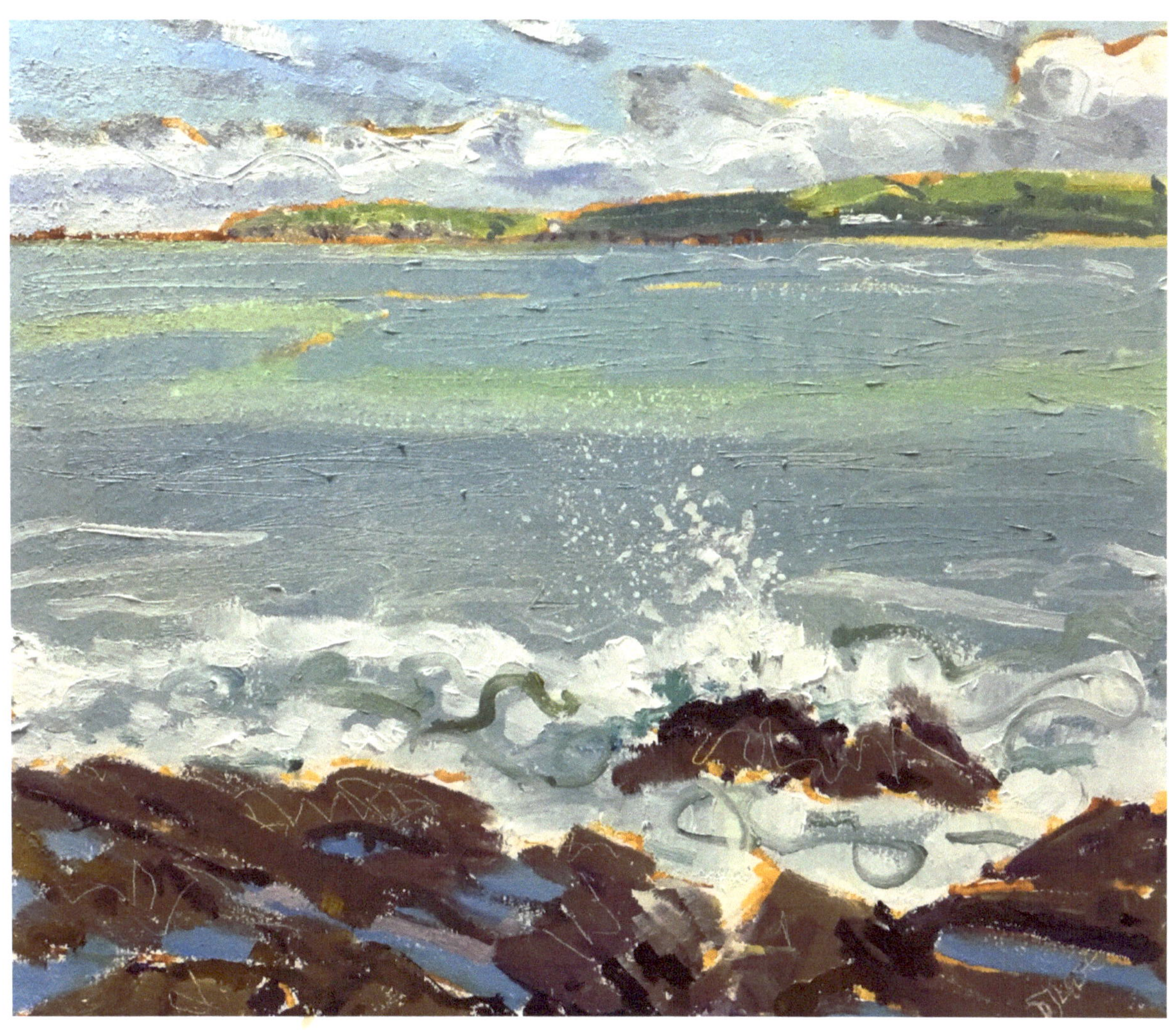

30/06/22
Paint Out at the Pier House
/// client.flag.damage

July

It was so wonderful painting in the warm weather. It reduced my kit by so much and made it so easy to walk to places to paint. I loved it in July. I loved being outside all year, but this was glorious. Of course things were not so green as the grass dried out and began to yellow and the 2022 drought began to be a worry.

We travelled to Porto in this month and the pochade boxes had to packed carefully to fly. The weather was similar to what was happening in the UK but a little hotter still and meant I needed to mostly paint early in the mornings to avoid the heat. The garden was filled with agapanthus which was amazing and a great subject to paint. I did do a painting on one of the days across the valley from a supermarket carpark in the village we were staying. Quite a good way of getting out of doing the food shopping!

06/06/22
Westward Ho! Beach
/// lively.tried.strictest

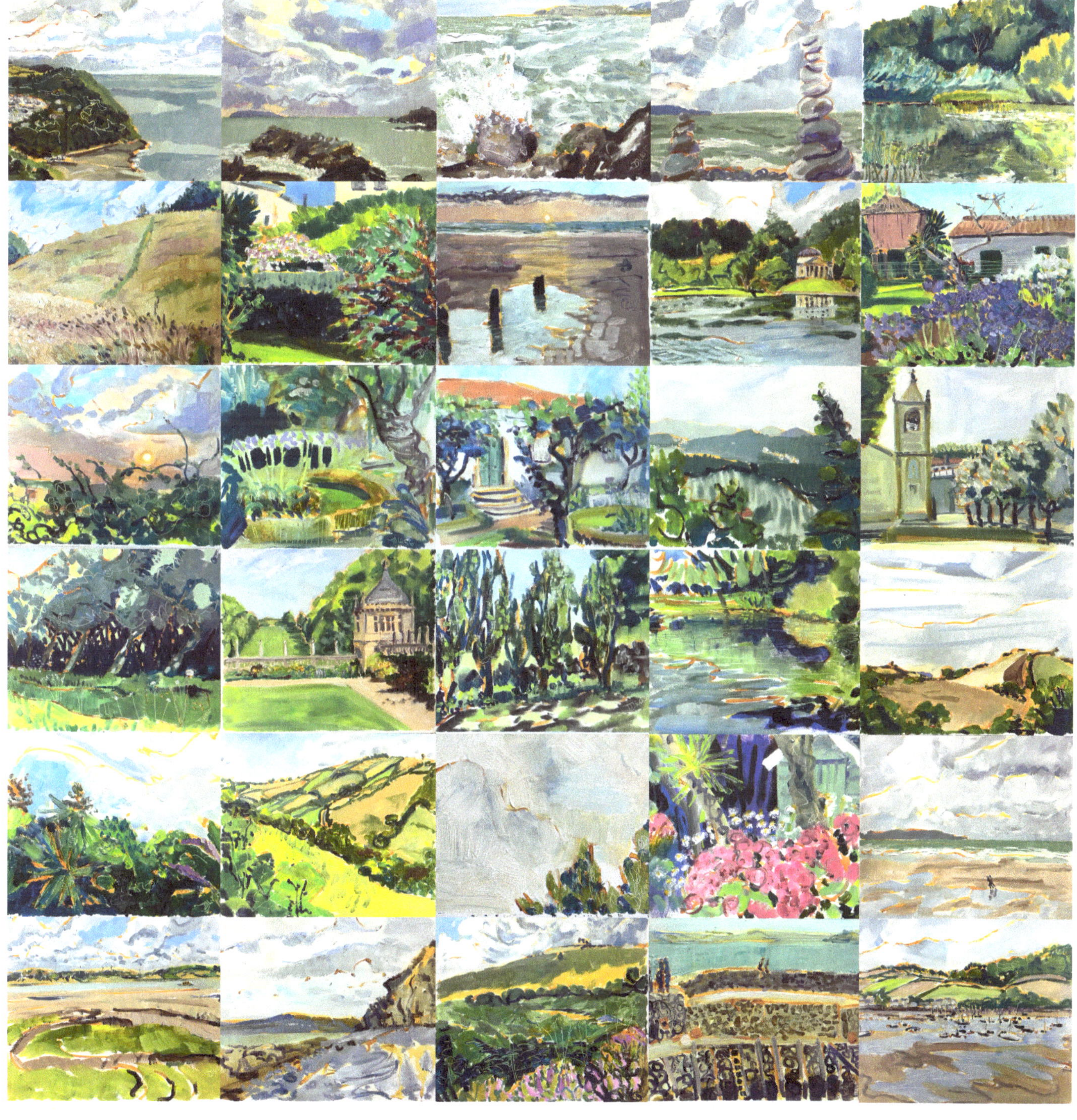

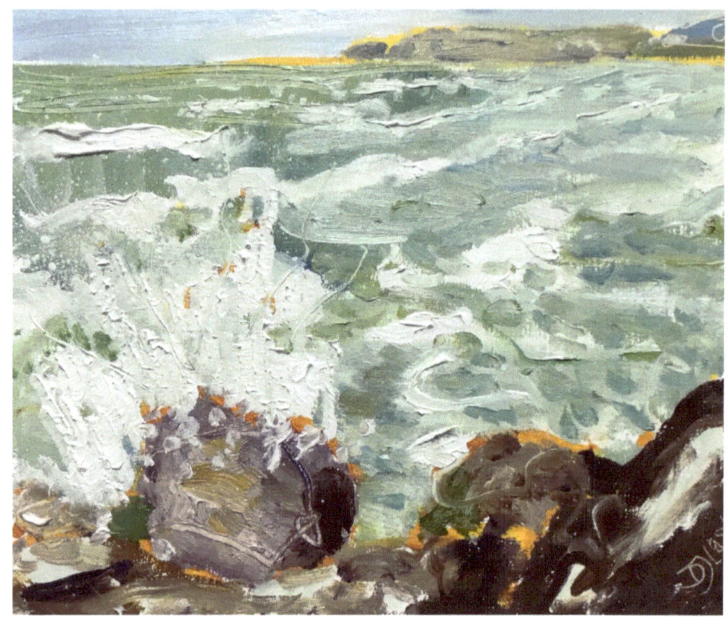

03/07/22
The Slipway, Westward Ho!
/// cherish.technical.amending

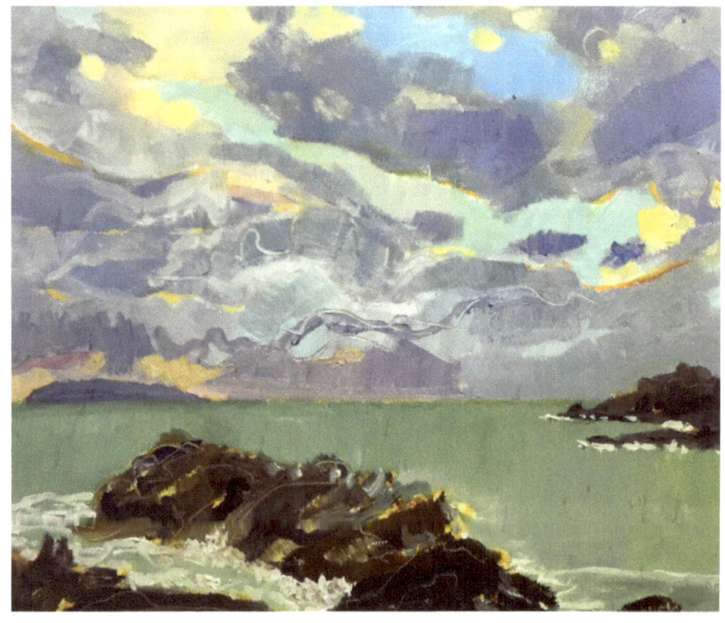

02/07/22
Hartland Quay
/// swanley.waffle.clenching

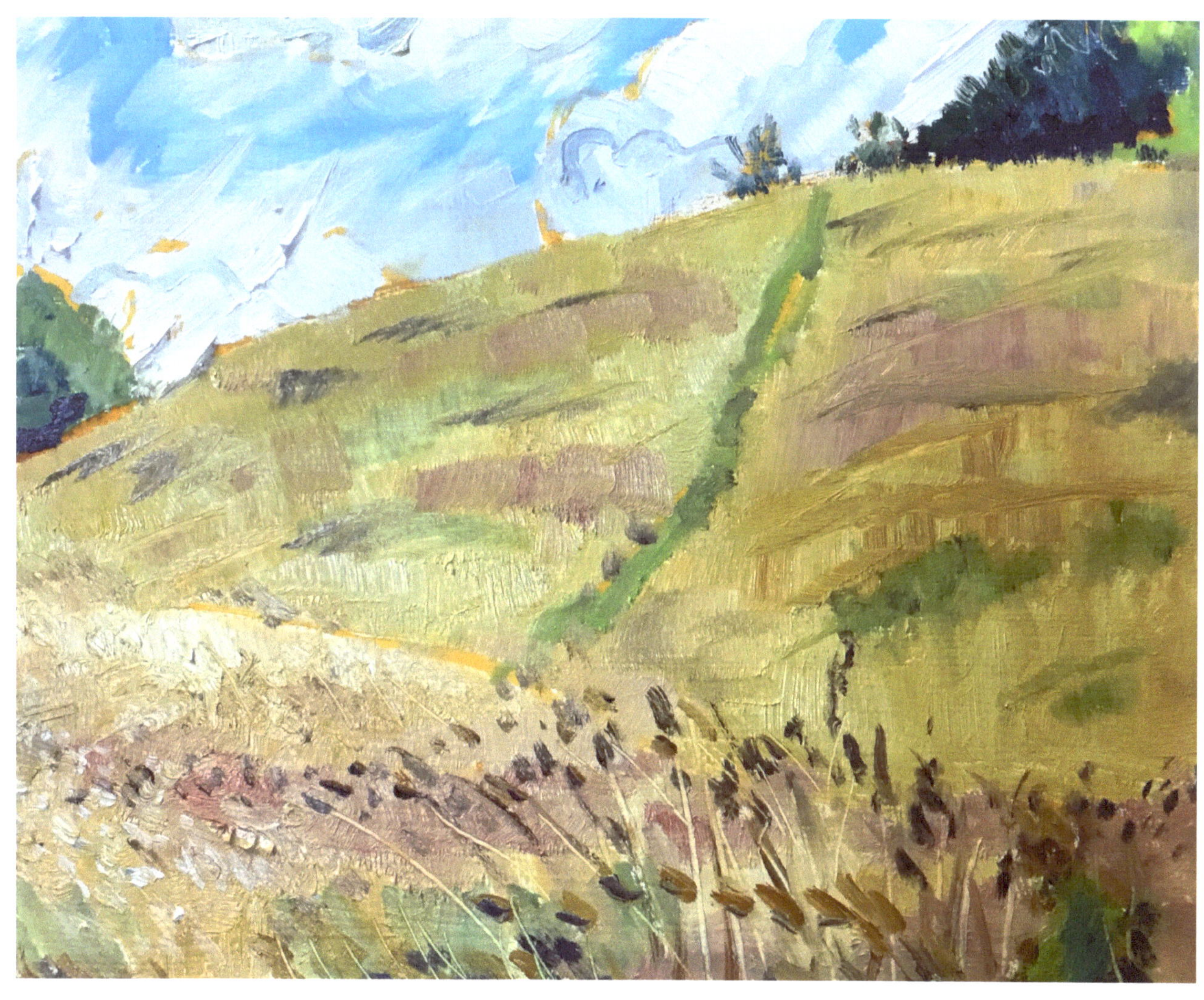

06/07/22
Meadow, Bideford
/// looked.usage.estate

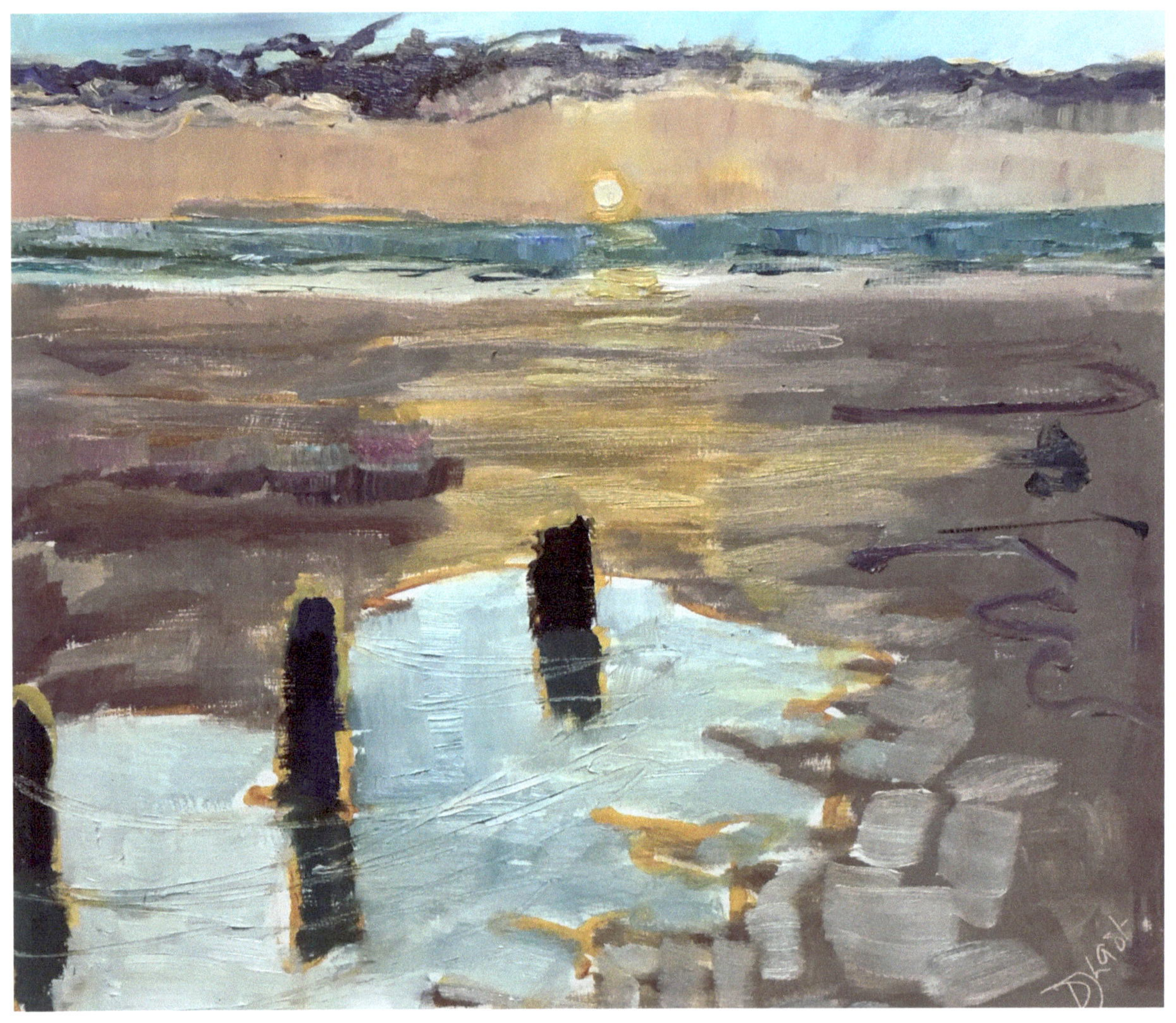

08/07/22
Westward Ho! Sunset
/// present.tribe.rhino

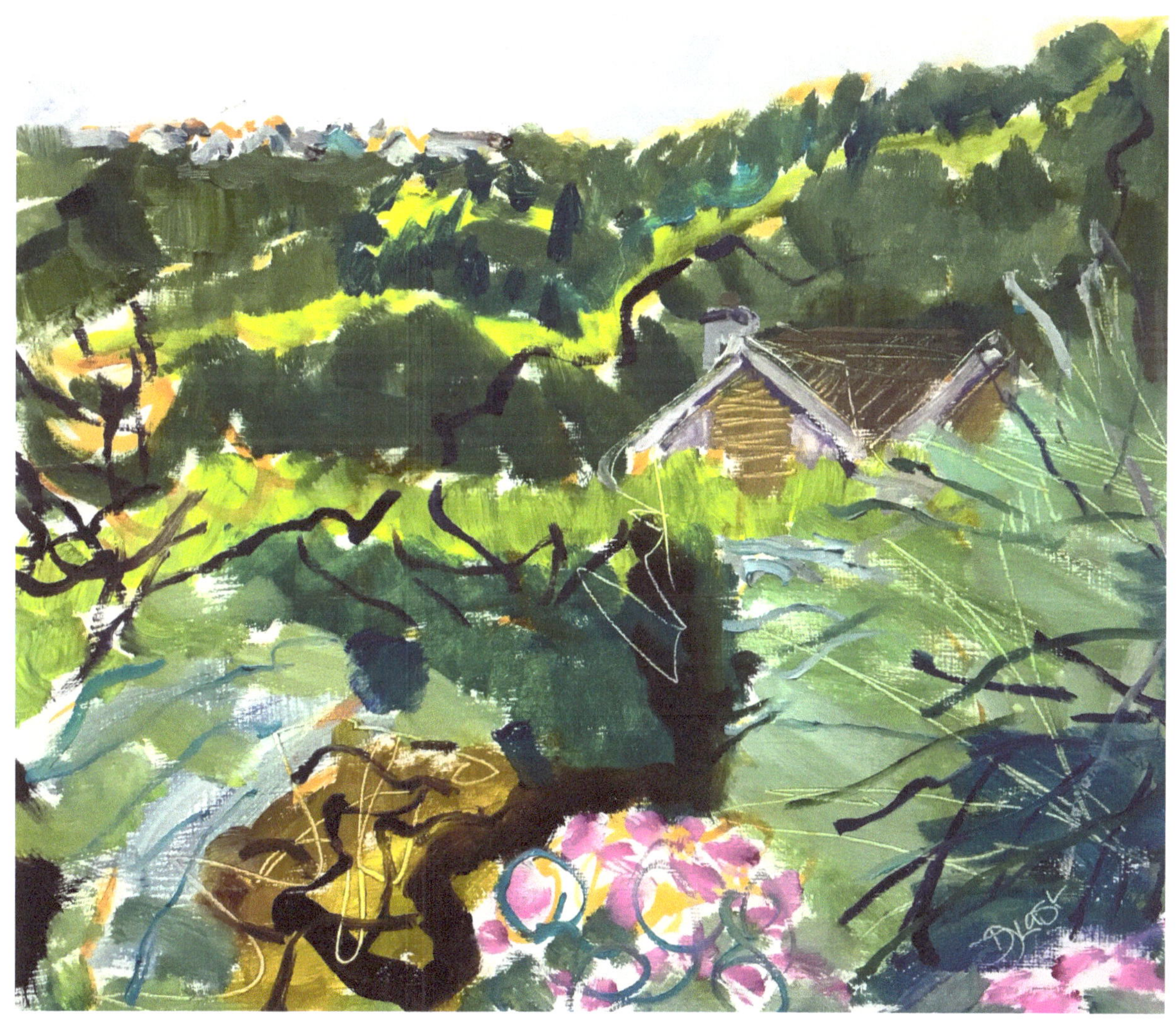

31/07/22
From the Pier House
/// moon.lucky.rant

August

It was warm still but the nights were beginning to draw in bringing earlier sunsets. The highlight of August was my artist in residency at the Artist Cabin in Bucks Mills. This glorious little cove tucked into the North Devon Coastline is the location of possibly one of the National Trust's smallest properties, the summer retreat of two artists, Mary Stella Edwards and Judith Ackland. I was able to paint there for 8 days, coming and going every day. It was a magical place to be and felt very inspiring. I was happy to open the cabin for others to see inside and it was so good to see the delight they felt at being able to be there.

What was most refreshing was to paint in different ways while I was there, not just the daily paintings. I did a number of mixed media studies which have formed the basis for some of the work I have been doing in 2023. The residency helped me to fully enjoy and give time to the Painting the Year project and not having to fit it in around other things. It helped me to see again after so many months the value of the project as a form of research and a record of my life for a year. As I looked at the paintings done by Mary Stella and Judith, replicating locations through my own paintings and photos, I felt a deep connection to the location and them as artists. It was a wonderful thing to do and I was very grateful for the friendliness of those living in the village while I was there.

12/08/22
From Appledore to Lundy
/// hostels.courts.performs

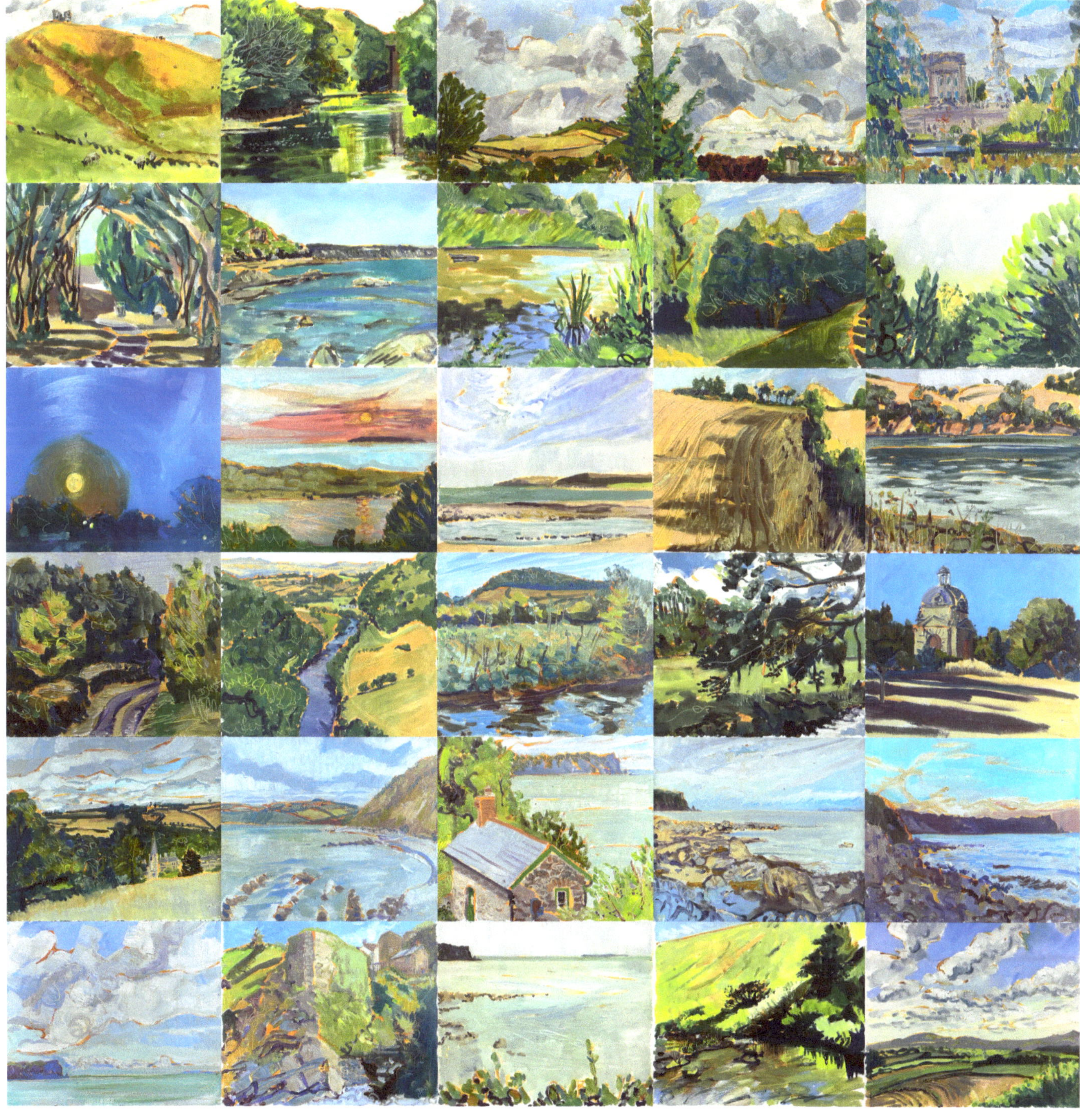

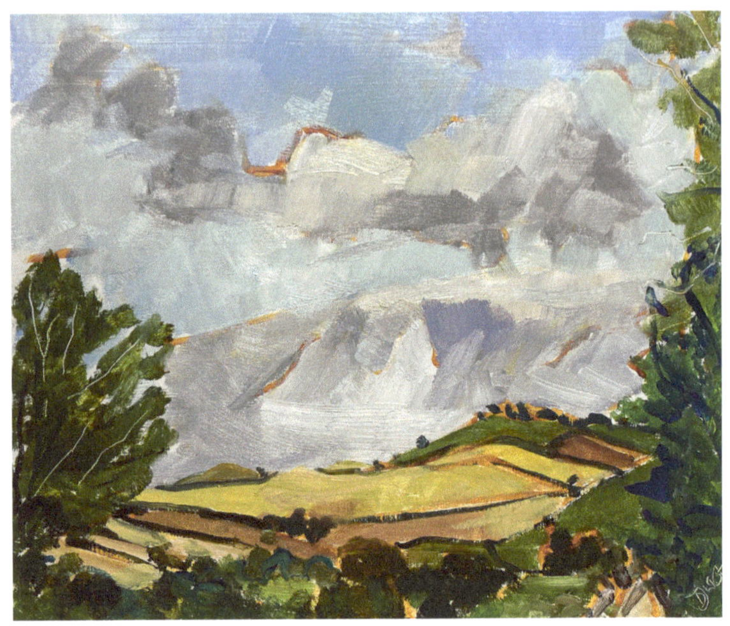

01/08/22
Northdown Road View
/// arrives.phones.second

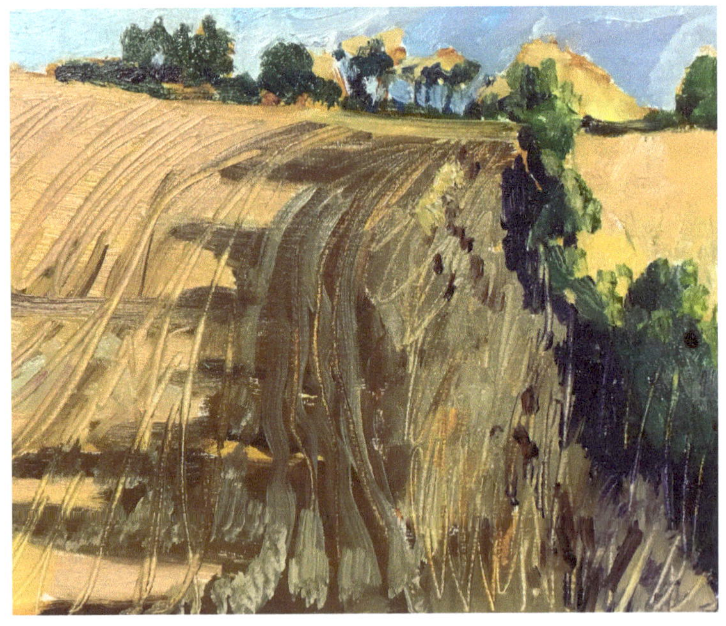

14/08/22
Harvested Field, Bideford
/// spring.humid.above

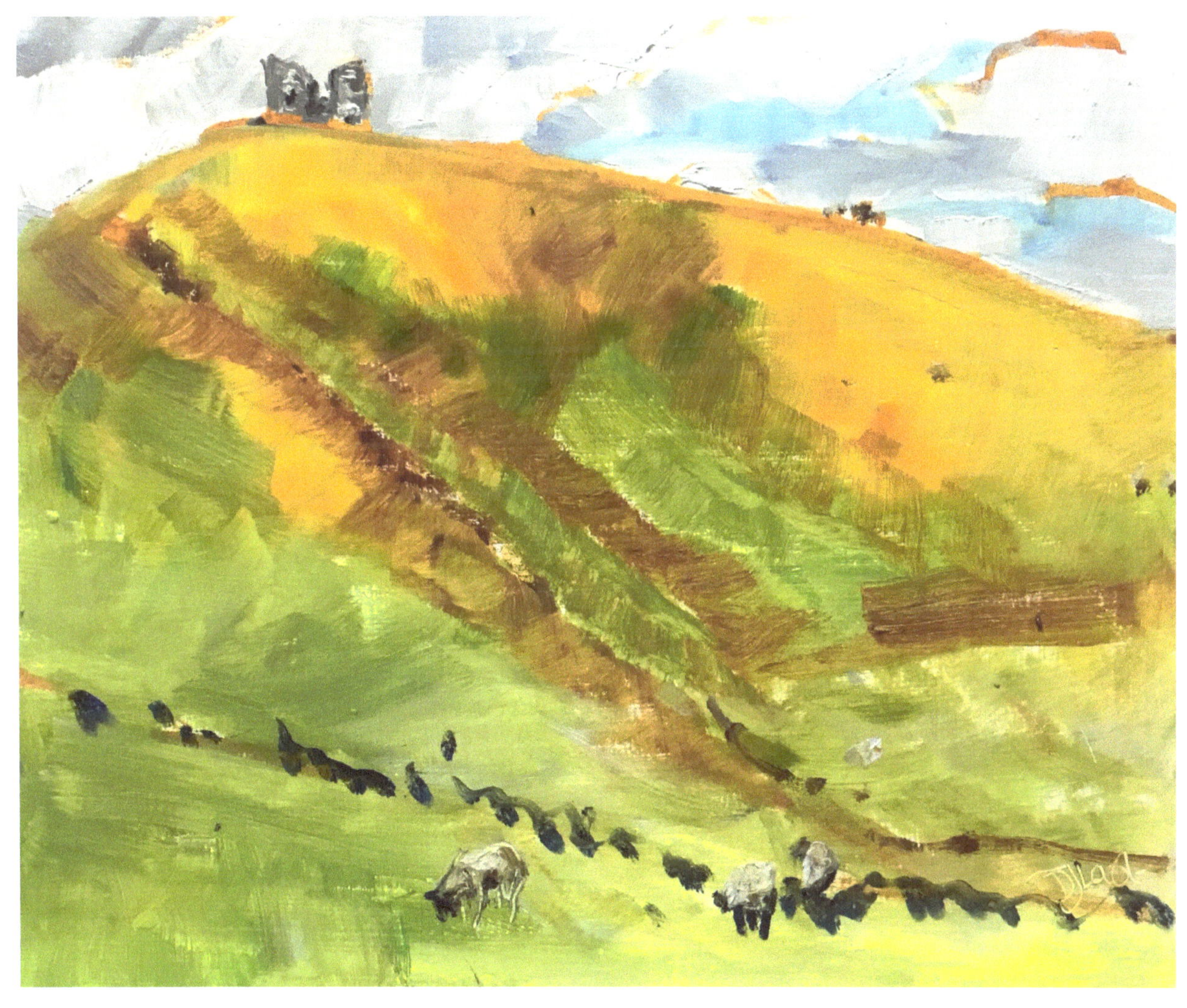

01/08/22
Instow Lay-by, View of Ruins
/// pounds.frostbite.recap

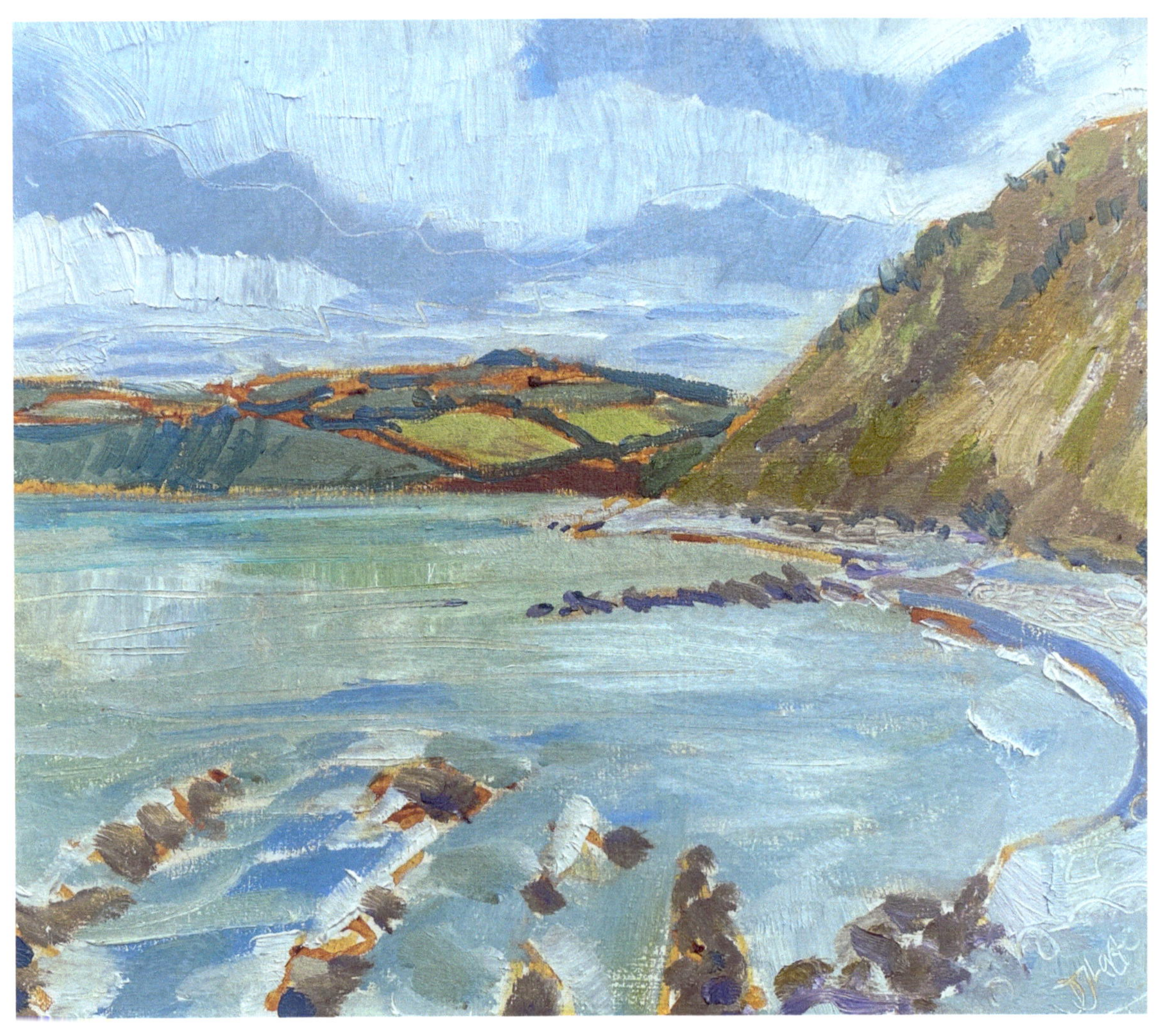

22/08/22
Buck's Mills Beach
/// intruding.upwardly.mailboxes

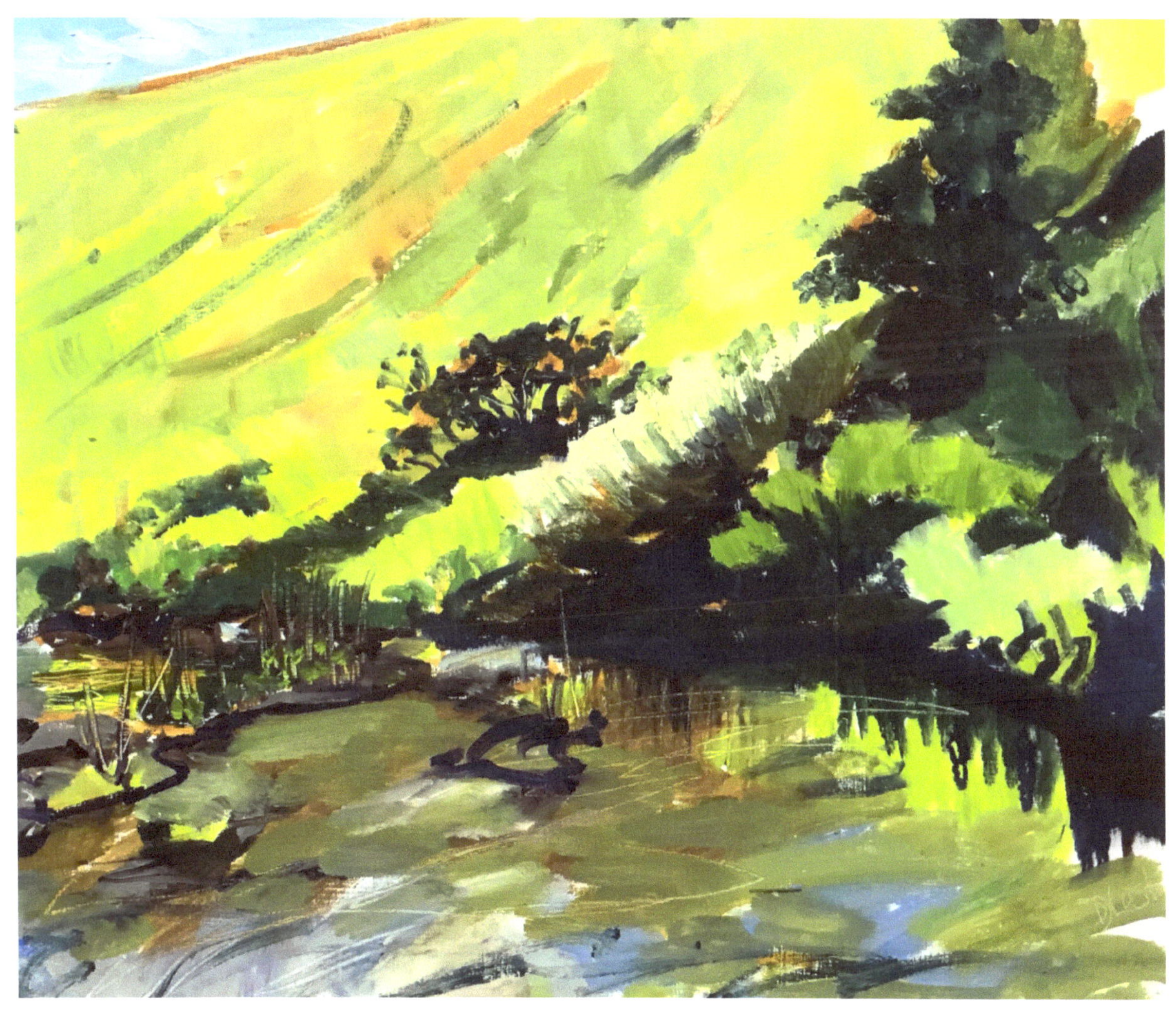

29/08/22
Simonsbath, Exmoor
/// update.shrimps.summaries

September

I was aware that the daylight hours were less and wanted to capture the last of the summer colour. At the end of the month, I was Artist in Residence for the Appledore Book Festival and was delighted to be doing this and included lots of en plein air workshops. What I hadn't planned for was that on day two of the book festival I had a call to say my Dad had had a stroke. Doing this project definitely had an impact on my family as we travelled around the country visiting them or at weddings and on holidays but suddenly this was a moment where the project might have to come to an end as Dad became the number one priority. I had thought about what I might do if I was ill and if there was a major family incident, but the reality was as complex and difficult as only these things can be. This was possibly the toughest month, but the paintings helped to pull me through. I really began to enjoy the colours of Autumn and the changing of another season. I think some of the paintings from this month are amongst the loosest and freest in the year, which is interesting.

12/09/22
Dune, Westward Ho!
/// edicts.tumblers.efficient

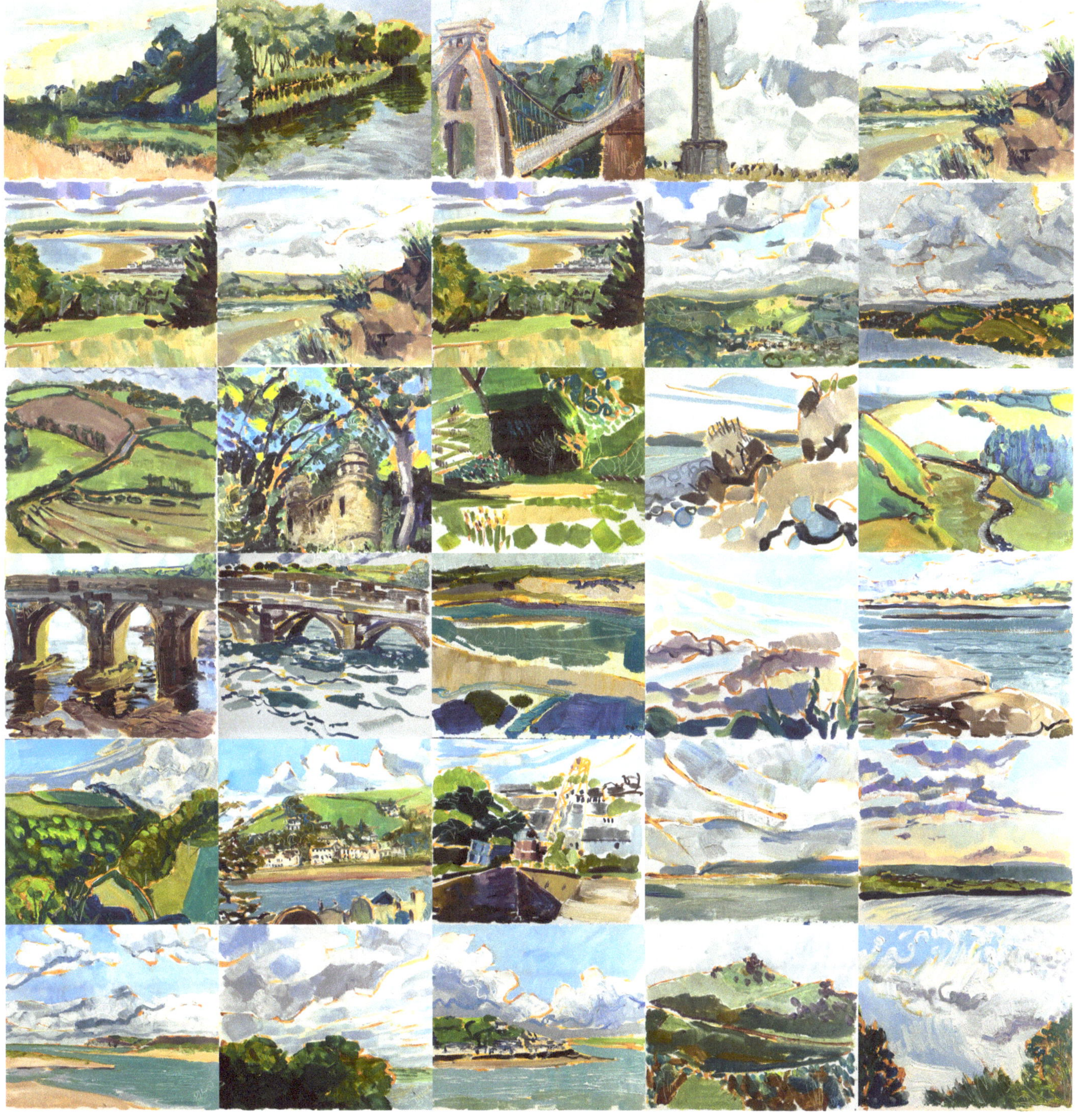

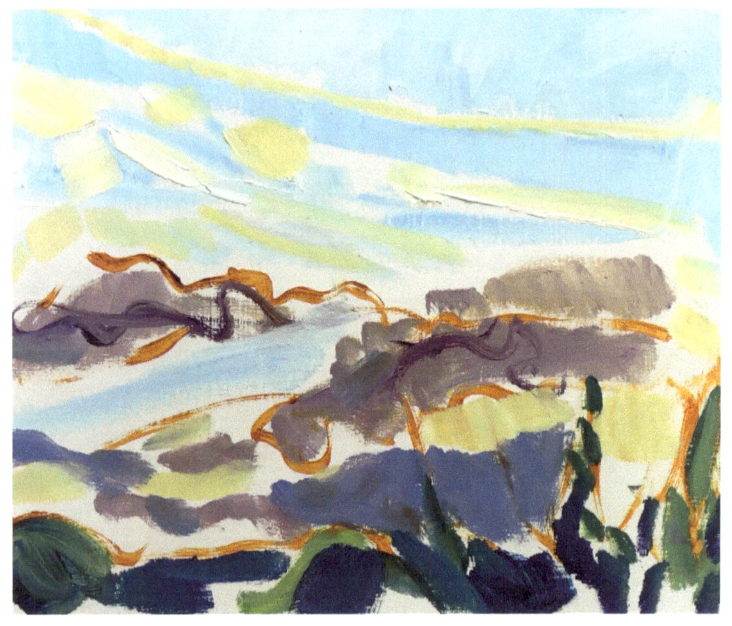

17/09/22
Evening Sun
/// pack.fancy.output

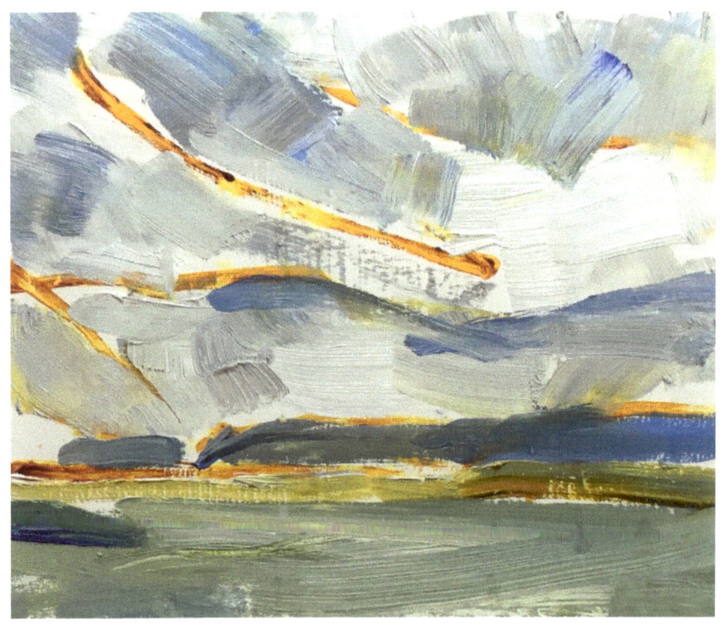

22/09/22
Skein Lodge Field
/// steeped.crumple.driven

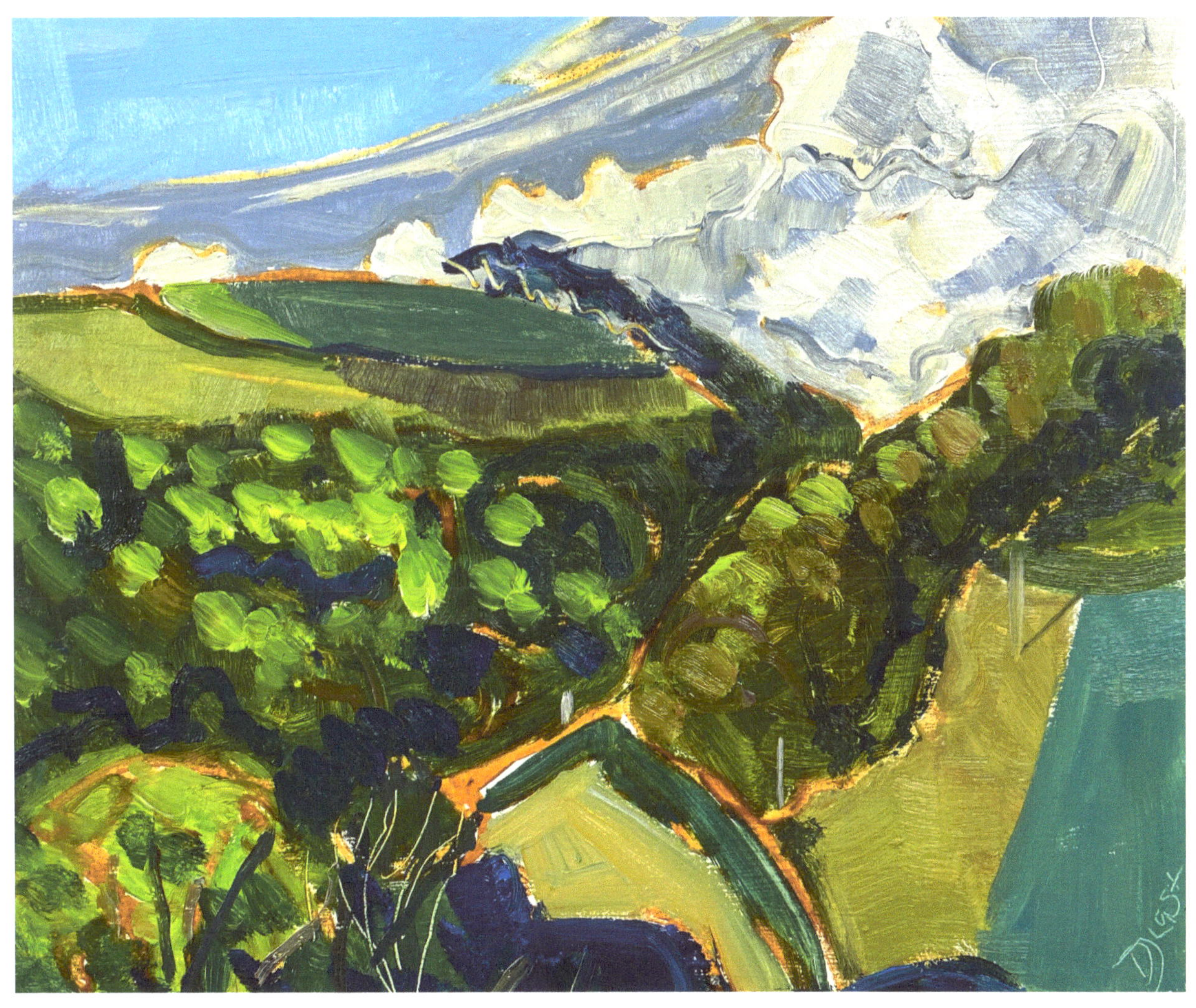

19/09/22
A39 Barnstaple
/// solved.dash.drop

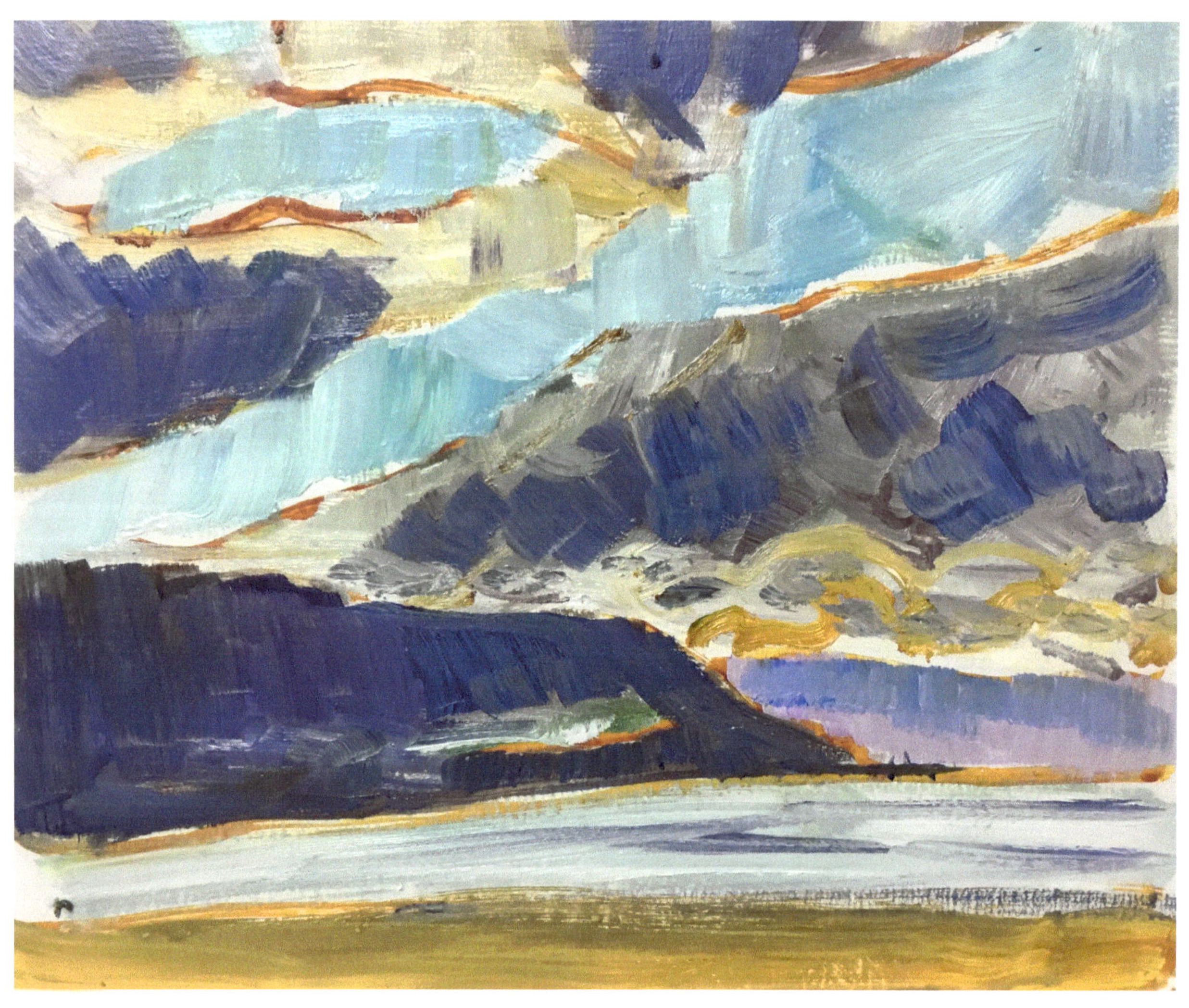

29/09/22
Westward Ho! Beach
/// stoppage.scrap.available

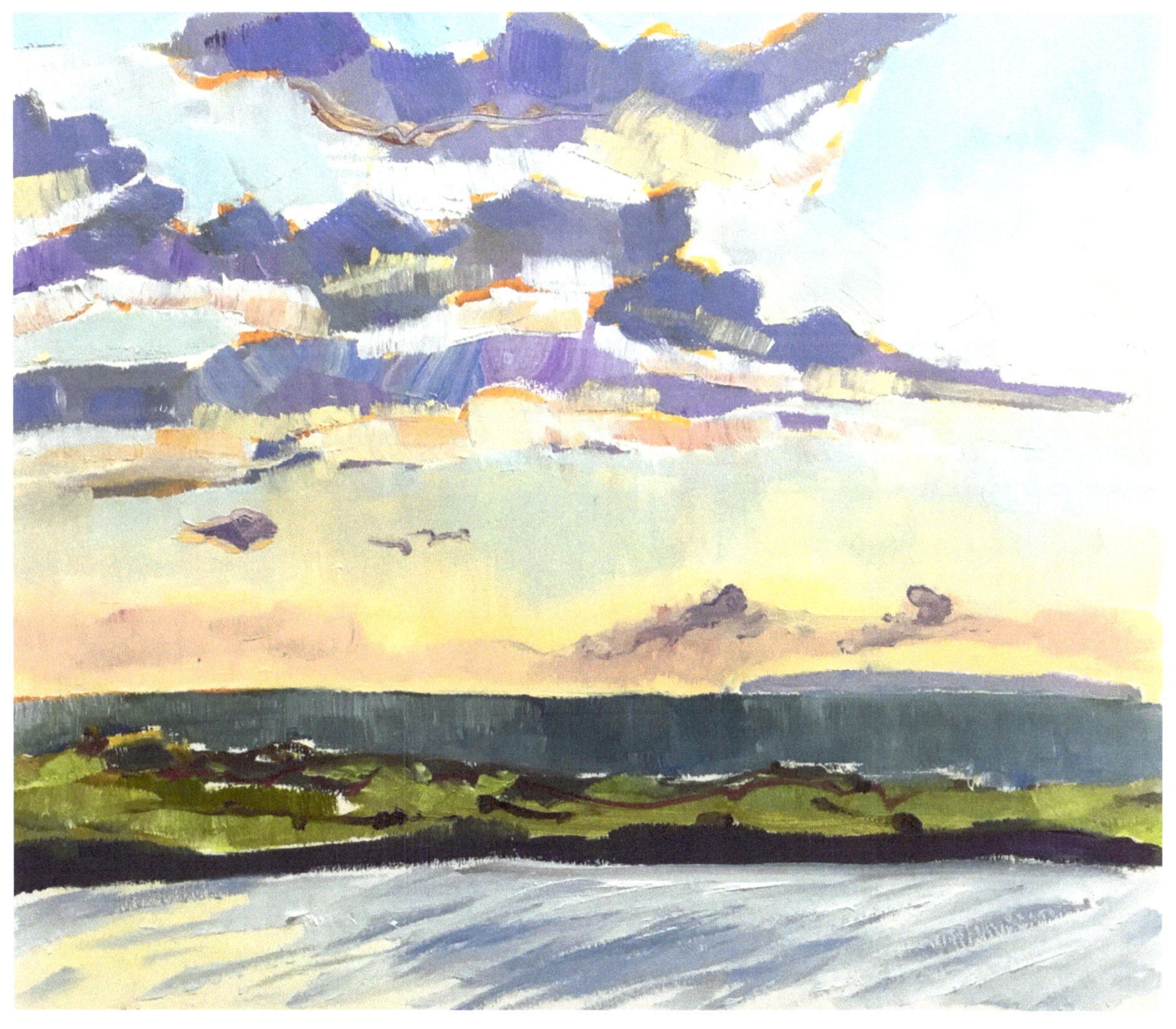

23/09/22
Skern, Appledore Book Festival
/// shortcuts.crowbar.flows

October

Autumn colours came fully into the landscape in October and I enjoyed the chance to use paint them. Under each painting was an orange drawing made with Quinacridone Gold, often done as a single line drawing. This orange line became distinctive in my style and was useful as I headed into Autumn. This was a wet month so my angling pod came into its own on several days in this month. I began to enjoy some truly dramatic skies and strong colours. As it was also getting colder I found I needed my winter painting coat on many days!

26/10/22

Kenwith Nature Reserve

/// driver.throw.email

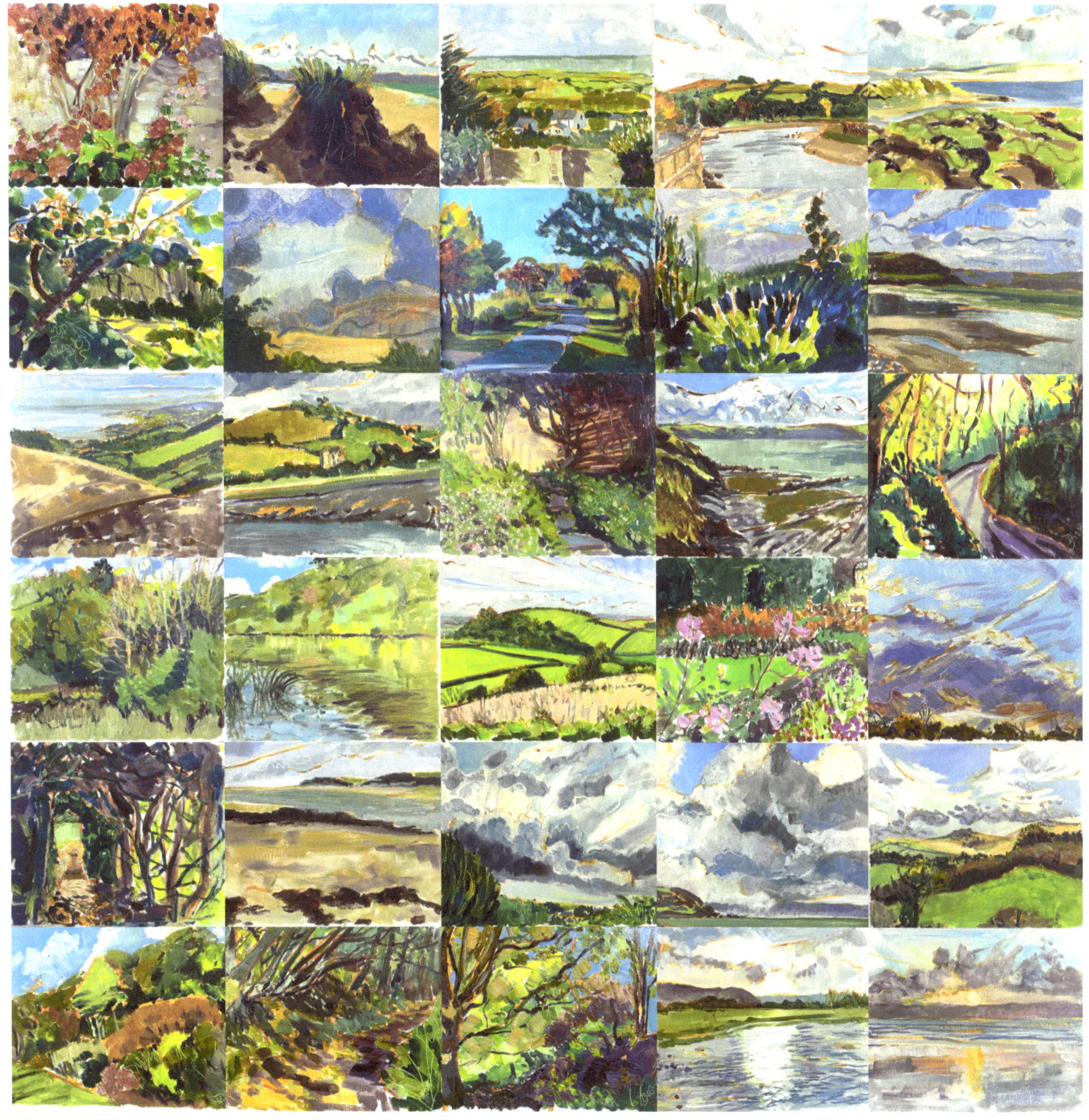

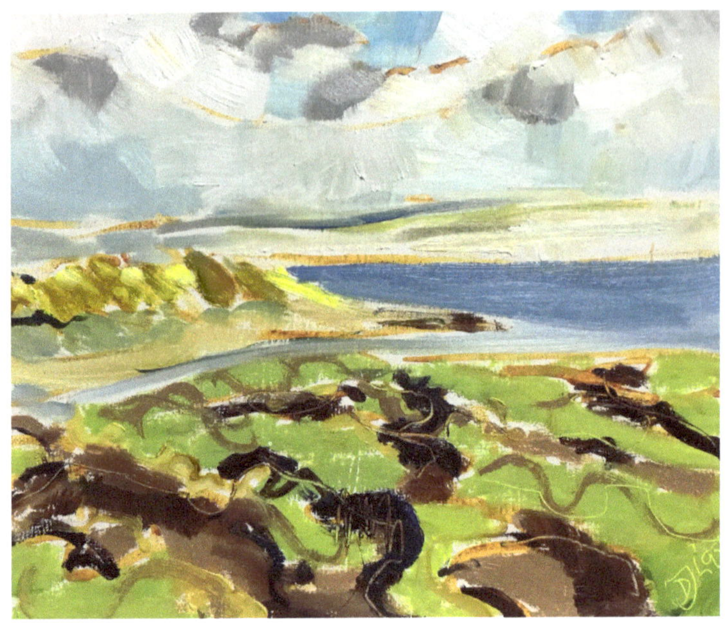

05/10/22
Grey Sands
/// driver.afternoon.breakaway

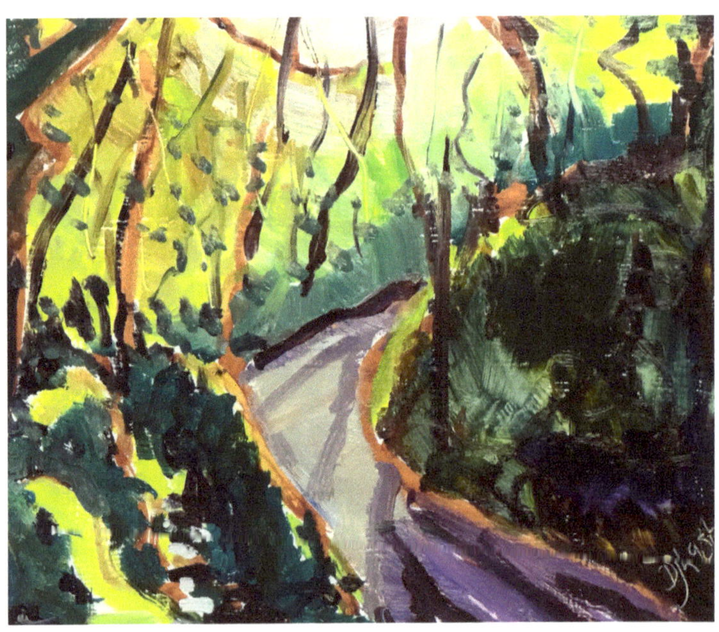

15/10/22
Bucks Mills Wood
/// readjust.erase.brozned

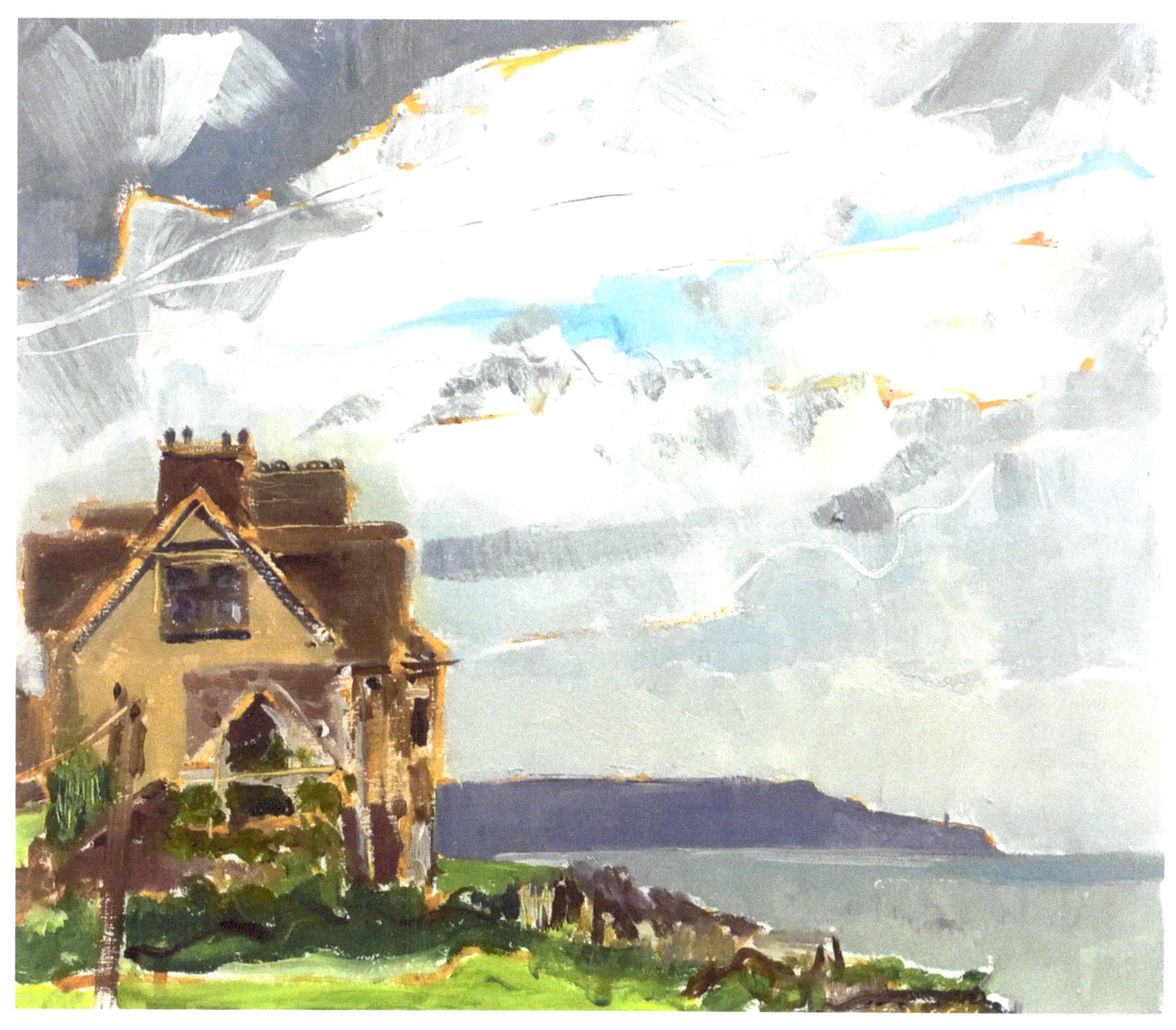

31/10/22
Spooky House, Westward Ho!
/// only.family.valve

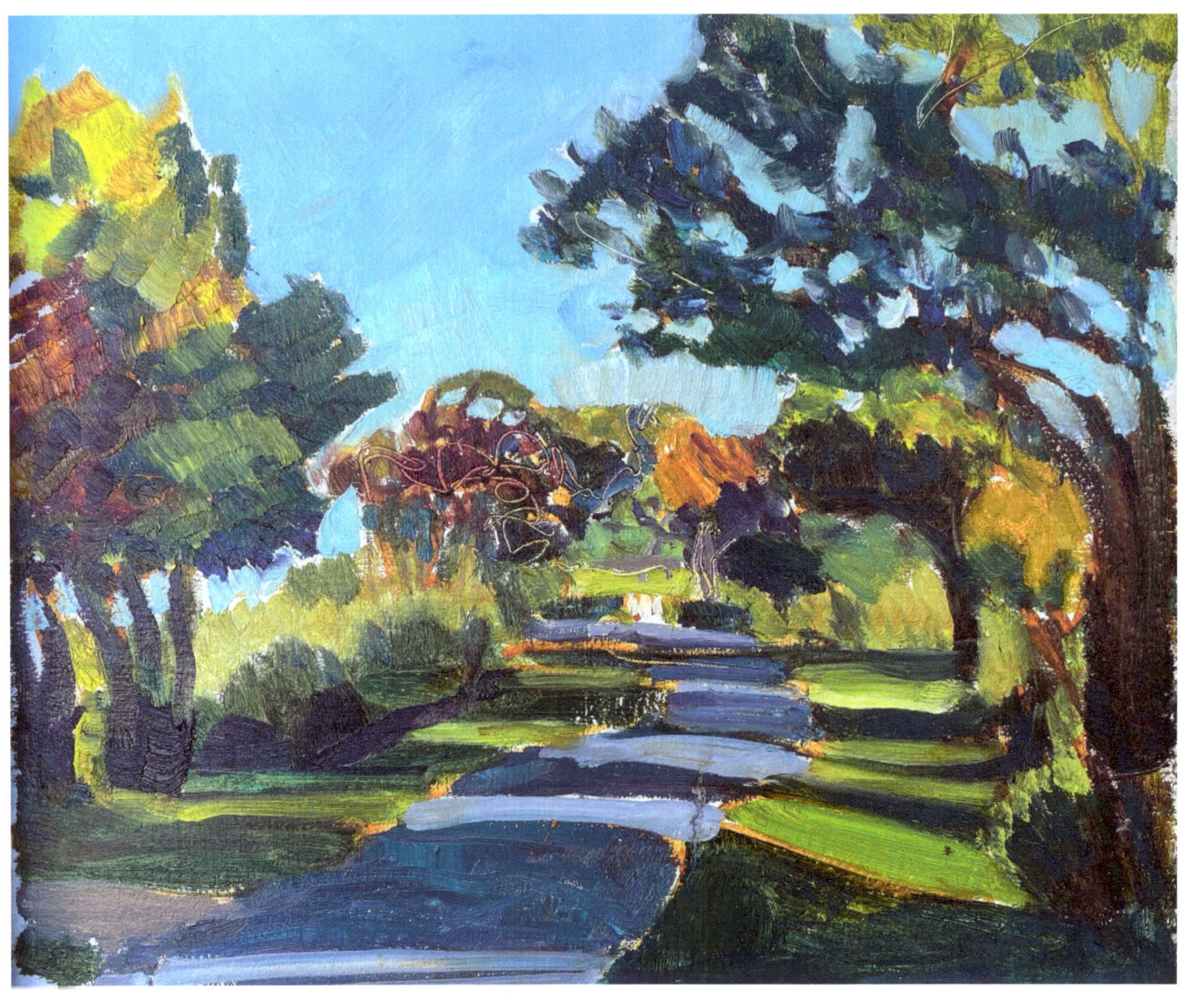

08/10/22
Featherbed Lane, Mixbury
/// handfuls.wrenching.gets

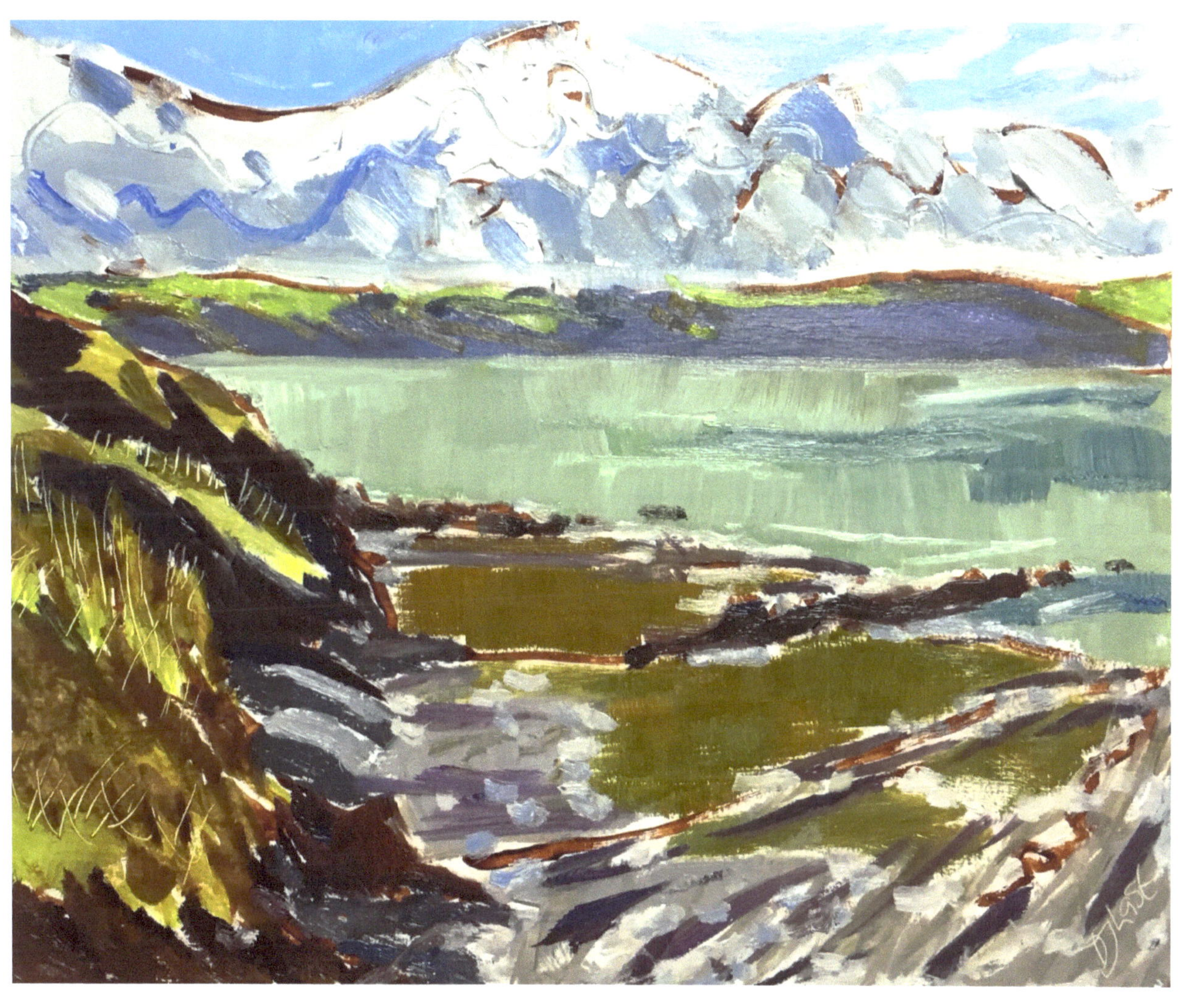

14/10/22
Abbotsham Cliffs
/// snowboard.lunged.shudders

November

During December I was literally counting down the days towards completing the project and I finally got the opportunity to paint snow in East Buckland and elsewhere. I was really beginning to notice how cold it was and painting on some days was a real physical challenge. It was fun to paint on the days around Christmas, especially as I had my family with me and my youngest daughter, Sophia, painted with me on one of the days. Throughout the year on the last day of each month I had organised a "Paint out at the Pier House" in Westward Ho! On the 31st of December a huge crowd of fellow artists, students, friends and family joined me to celebrate the successful completion of the project. This was a joyful and memorable event made even more fun with a few bottles of Prosecco!

09/11/22
Sunrise, Bideford
/// moved.puddles.bunks

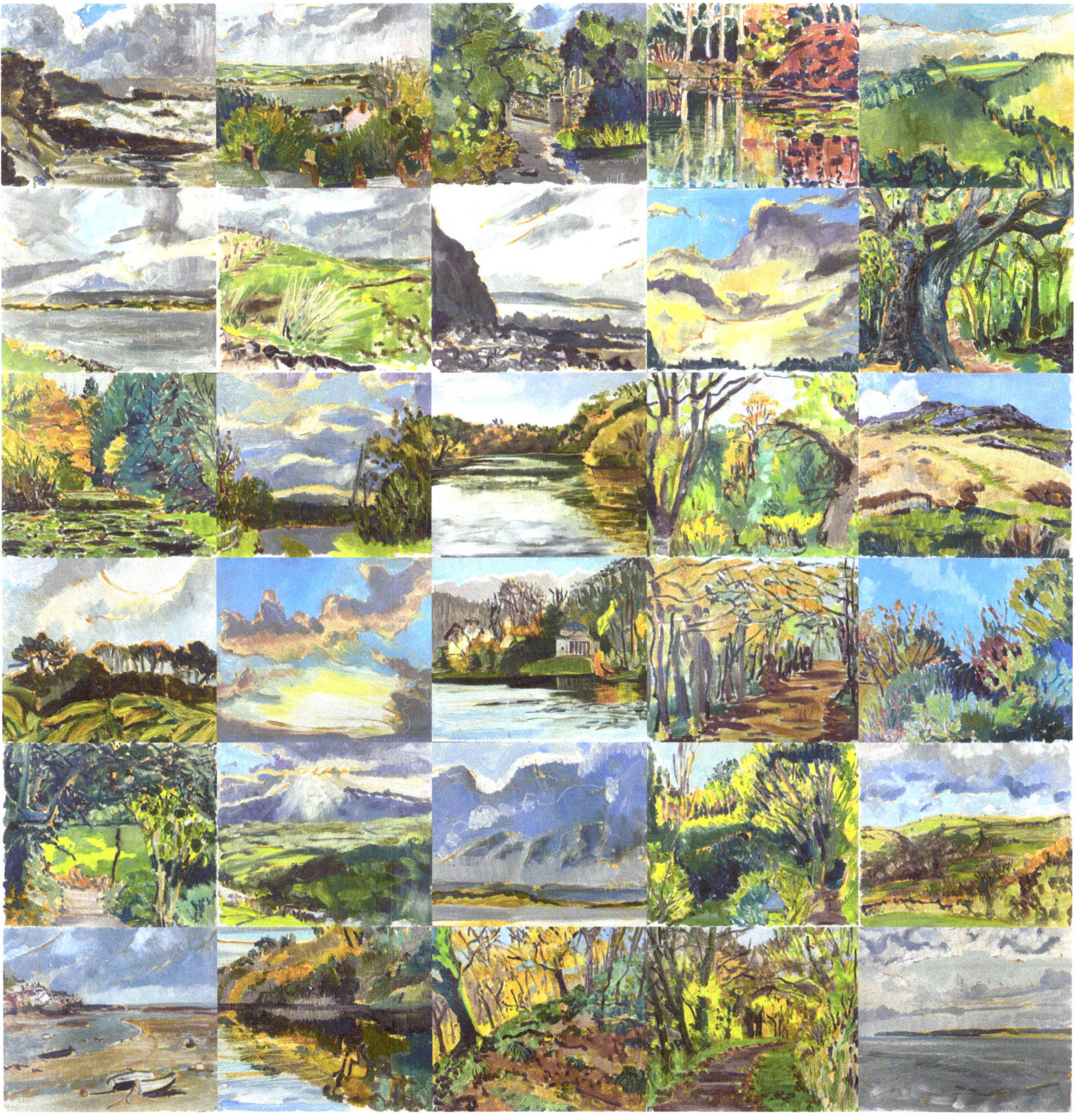

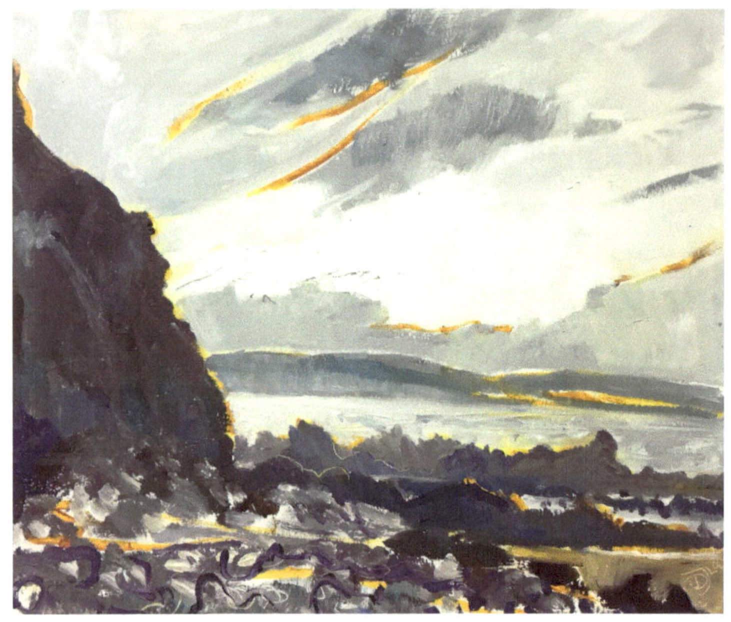

08/11/22
Duckpool
/// flown.scribbled.beans

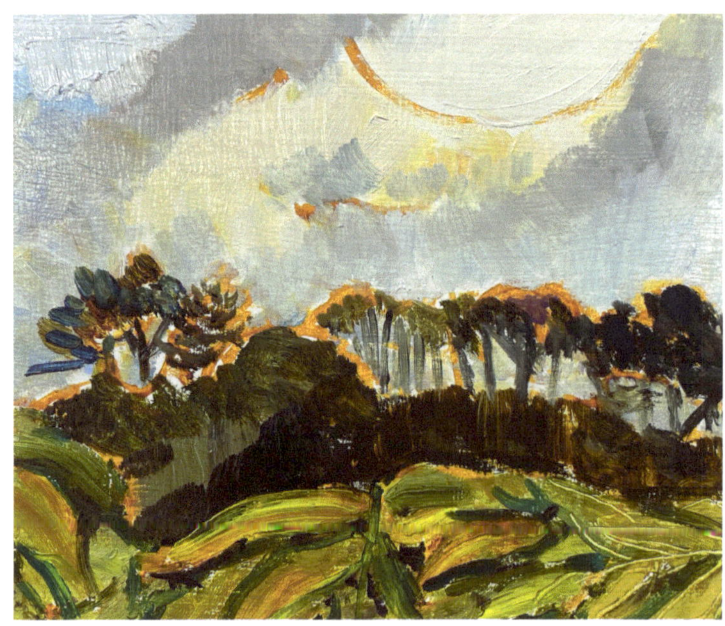

16/11/22
Horizon Trees
/// office.food.open

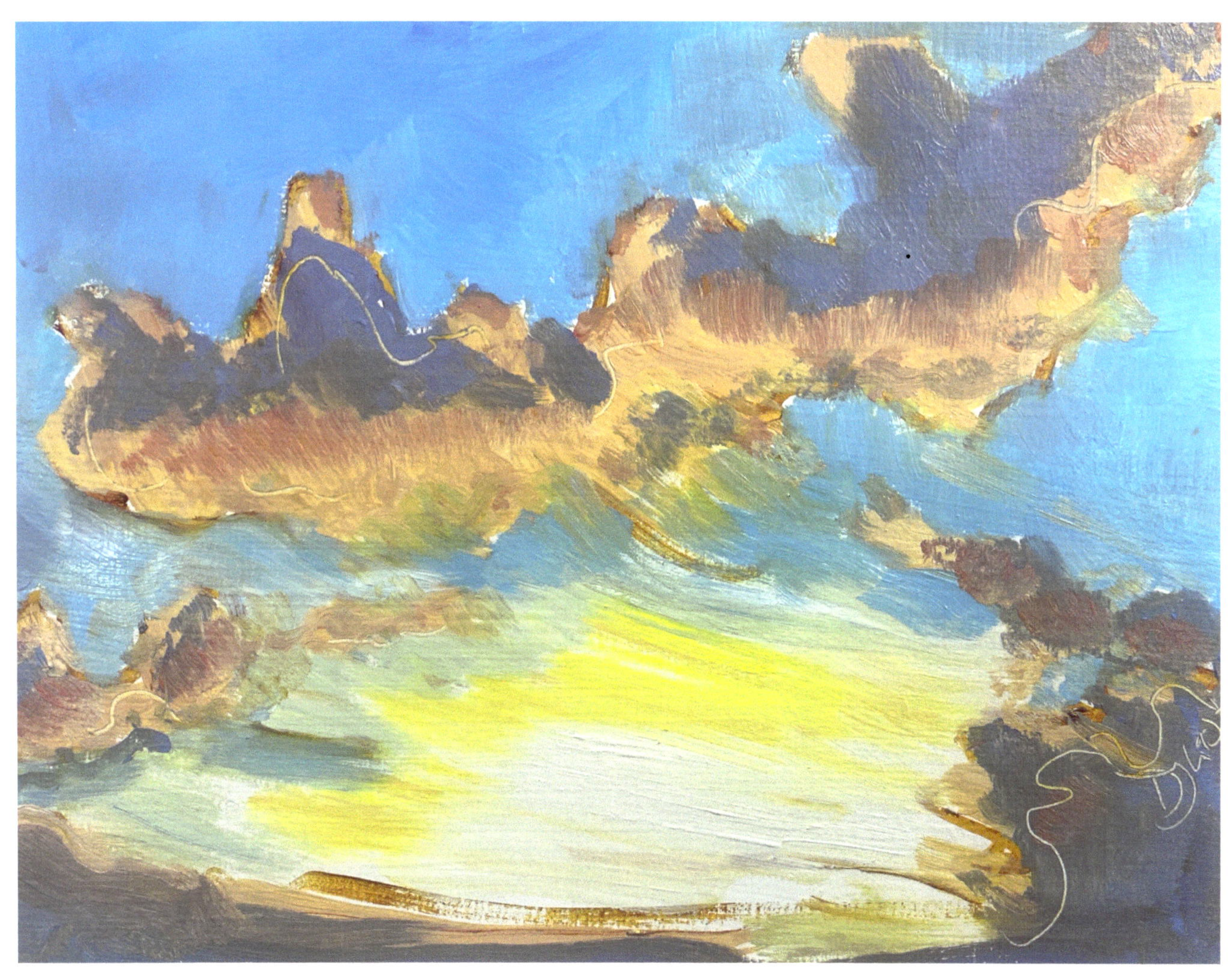

17/11/22
Sunrise in the Garden
/// office.food.open

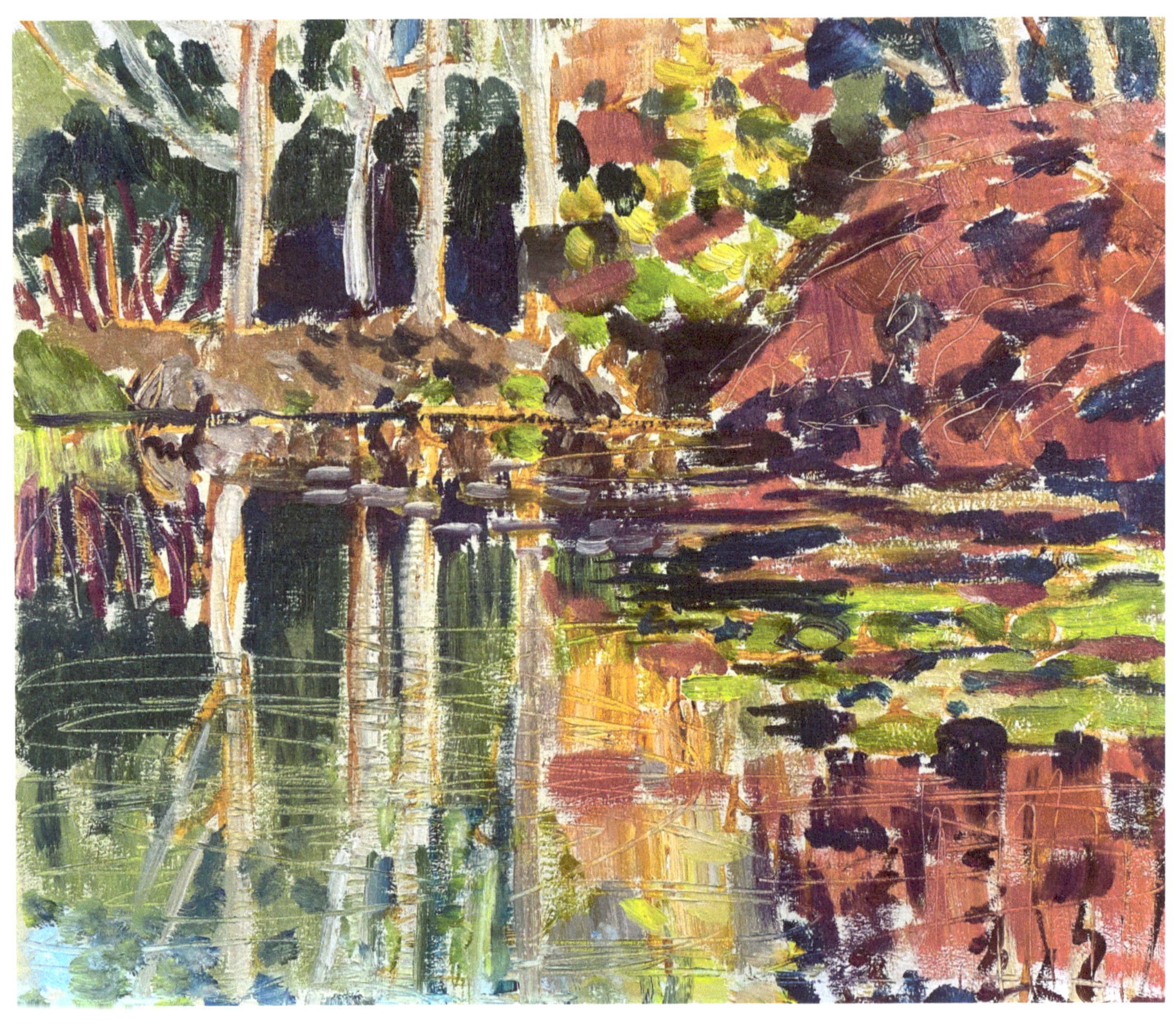

04/11/22
Rosemoor Lake
/// craftsman.latitudes.cello

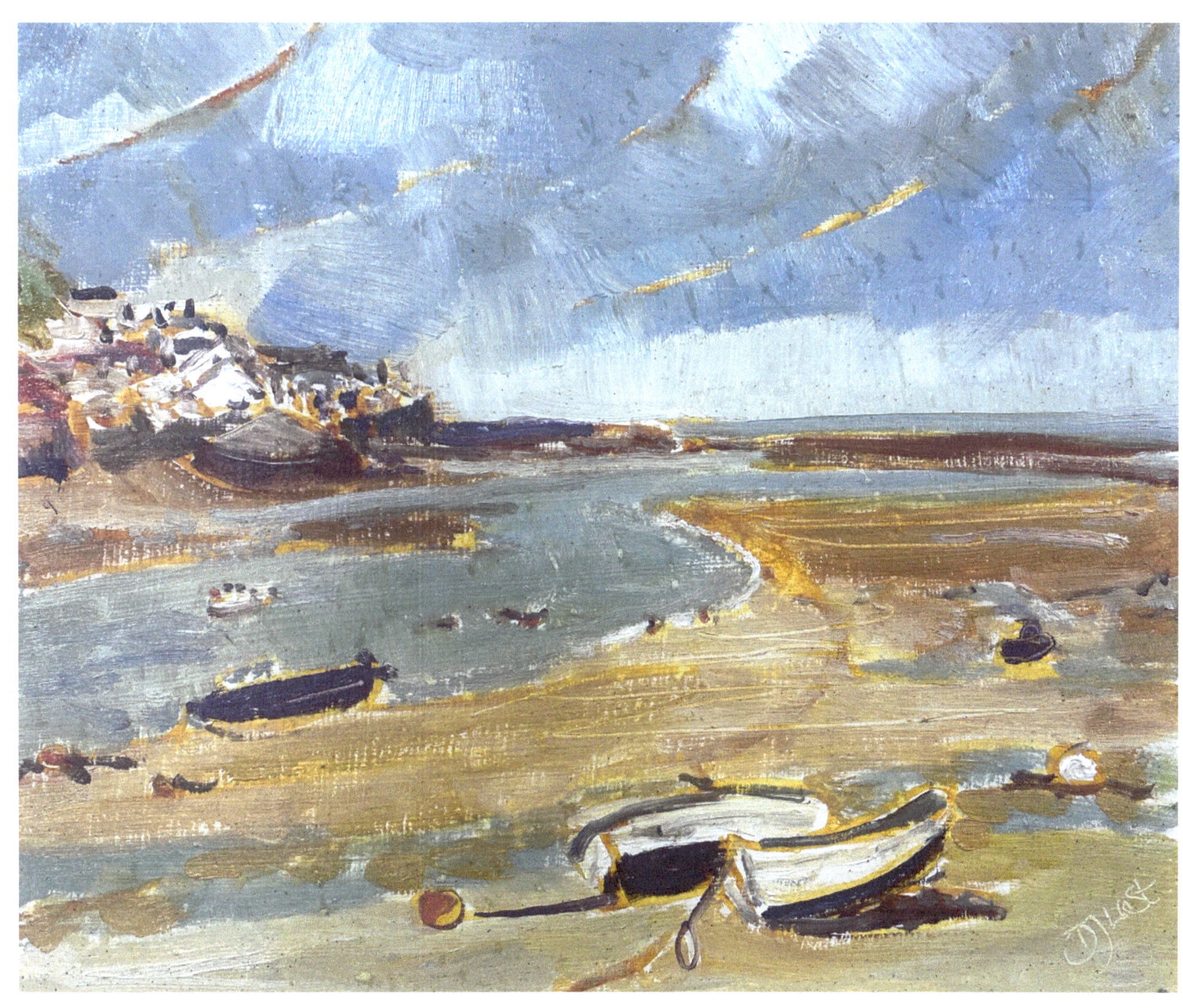

26/11/22
Instow Beach
/// awakening.pigment.panoramic

December

Autumn colours came fully into the landscape in October and I enjoyed the chance to use paint them. Under each painting was an orange drawing made with Quinacridone Gold, often done as a single line drawing. This orange line became distinctive in my style and was useful as I headed into Autumn. This was a wet month so my angling pod came into its own on several days in this month. I began to enjoy some truly dramatic skies and strong colours. As it was also getting colder I found I needed my winter painting coat on many days!

29/12/22
Sunrise
/// office.food.open

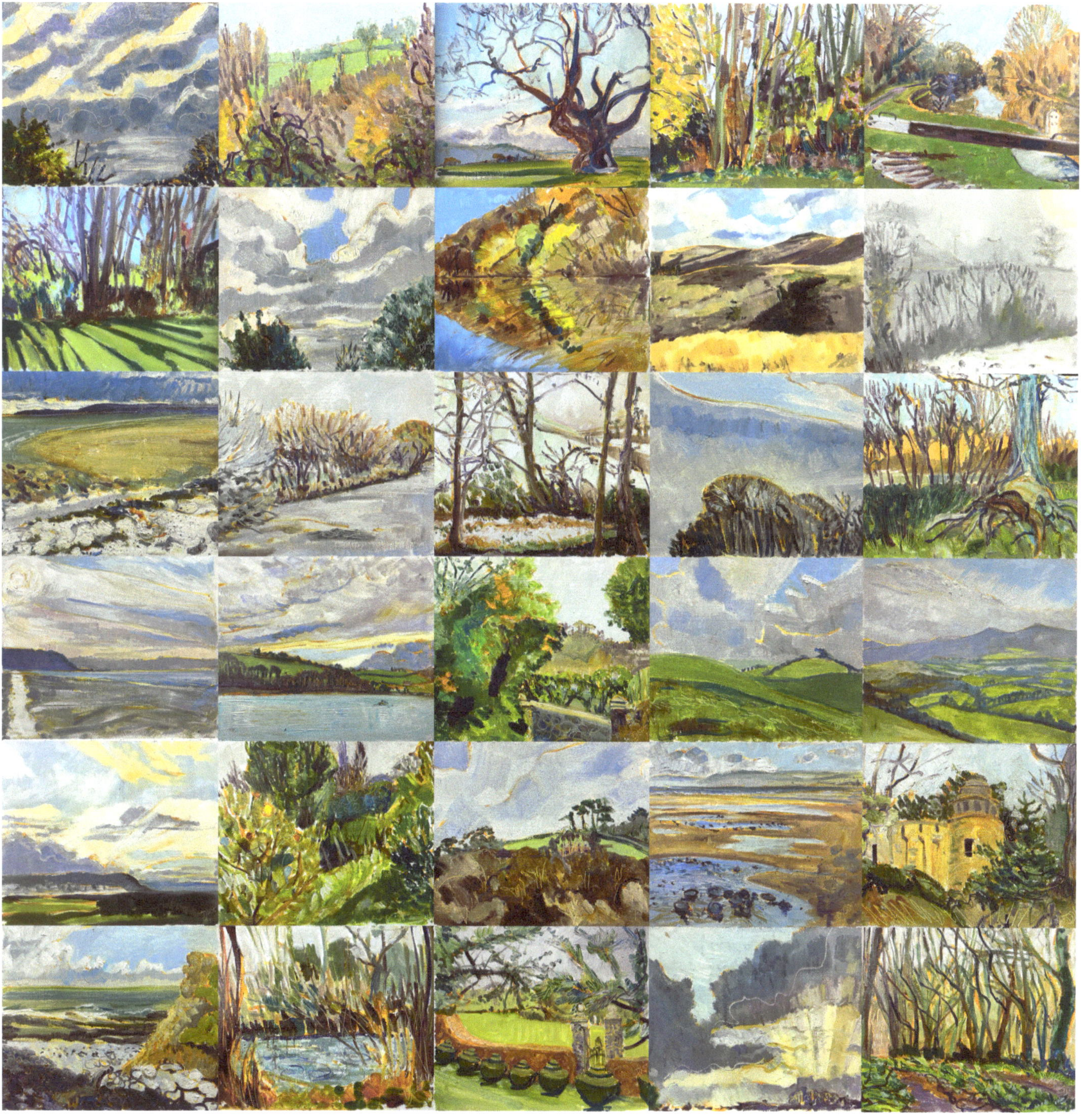

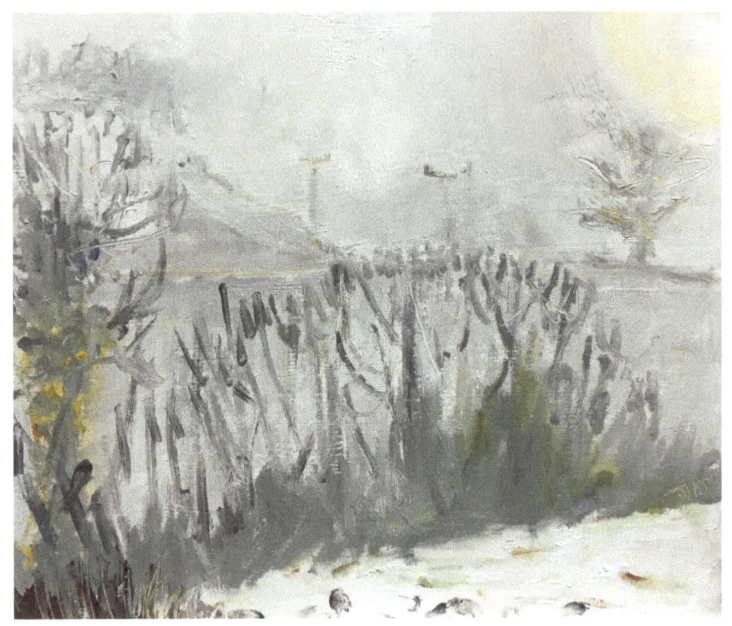

10/12/22
East Buckland
/// skipped.funky.bulge

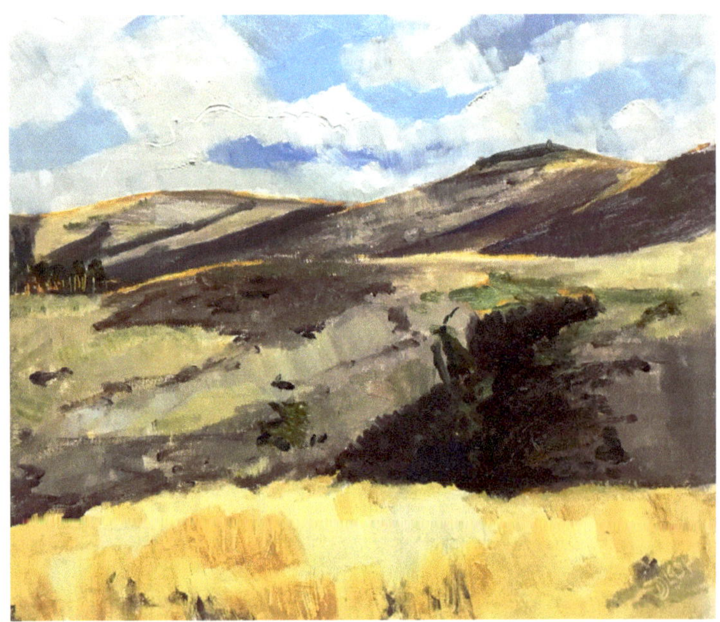

02/12/22
View of Dunkery Beacon, Exmoor
/// shades.vipers.clenching

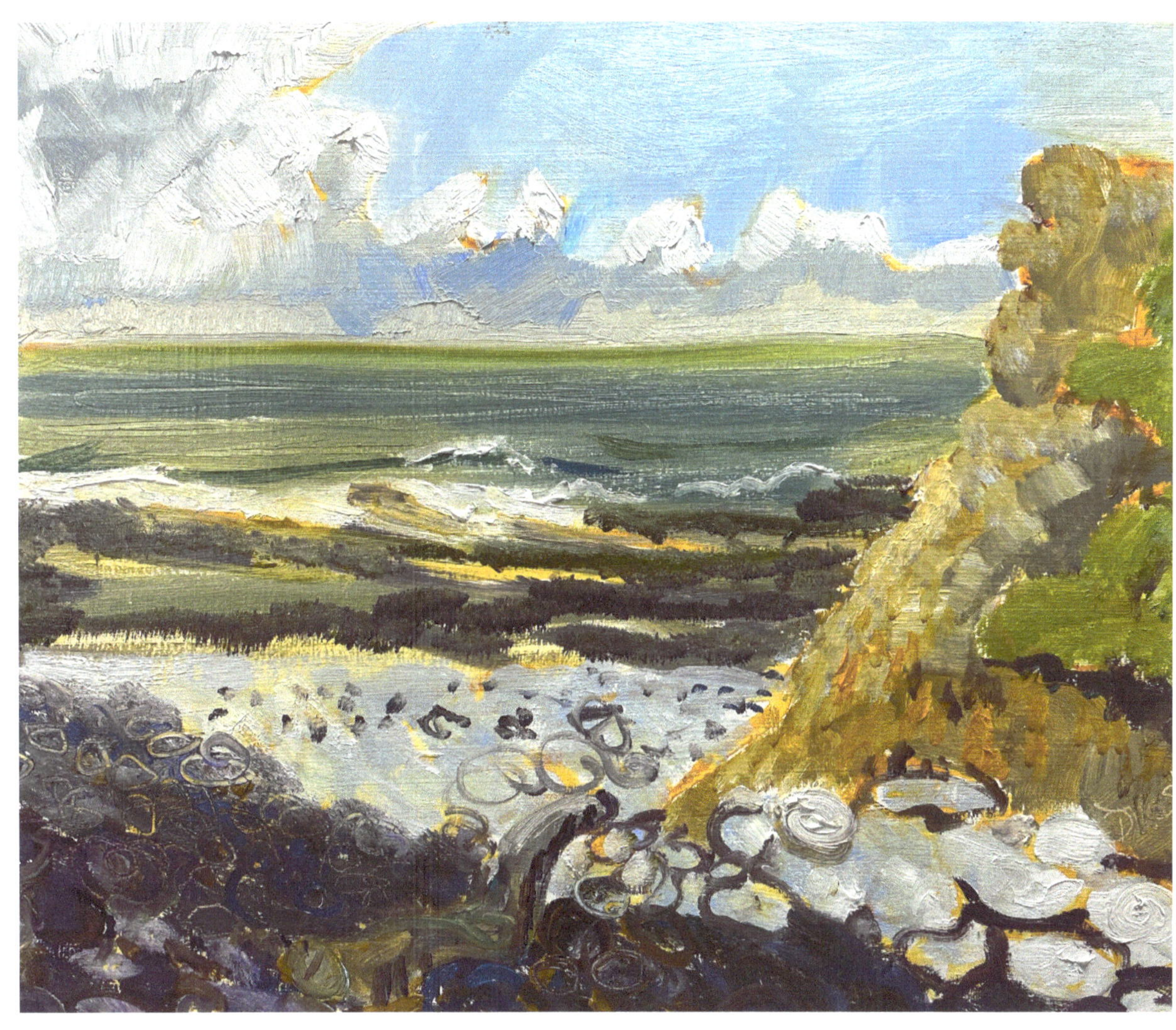

26/12/22
Abbotsham Beach
/// translate.skippers.bookshelf

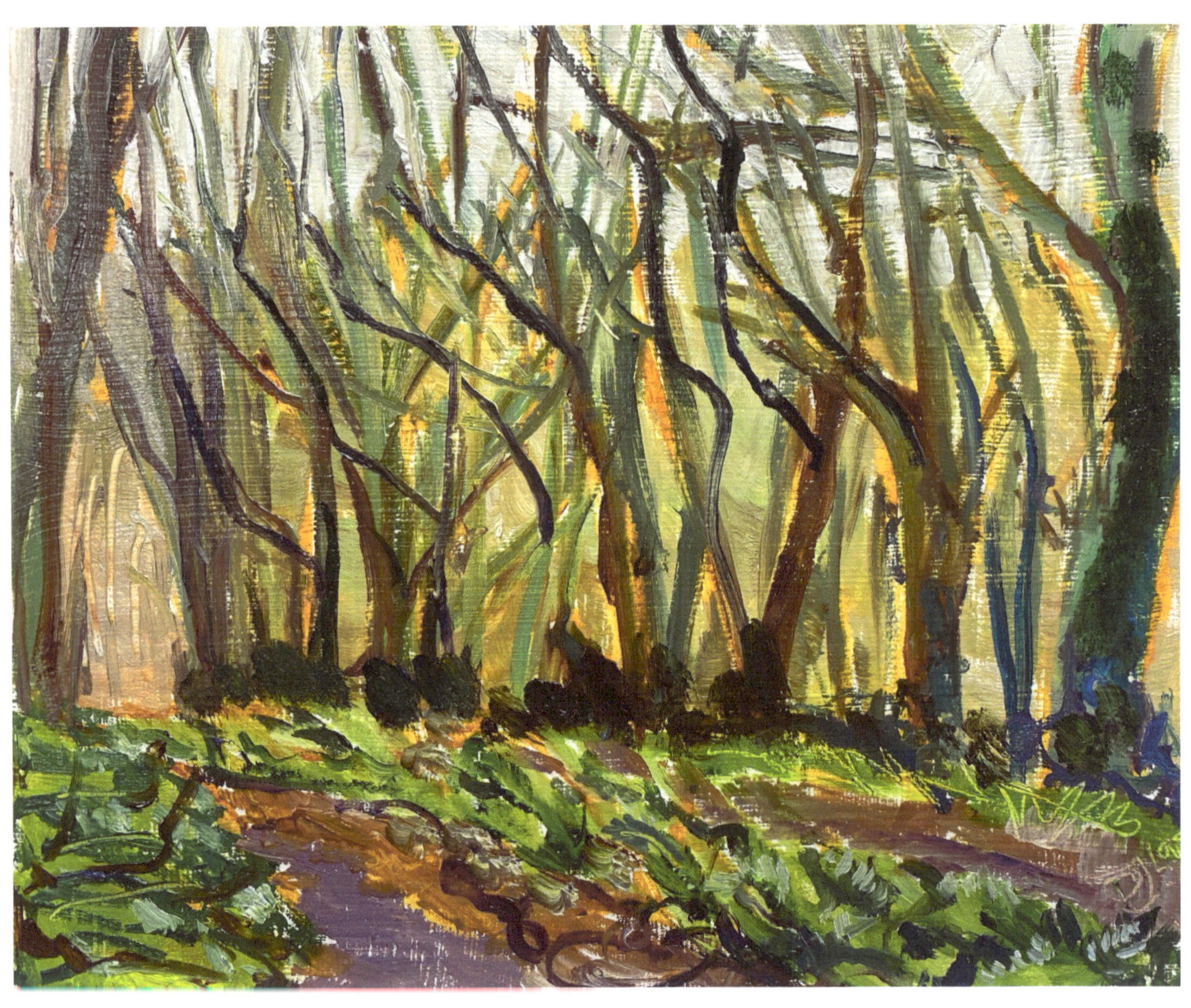

30/12/22
Tarka Trail, Torrington
/// fenced.townhouse.snacks

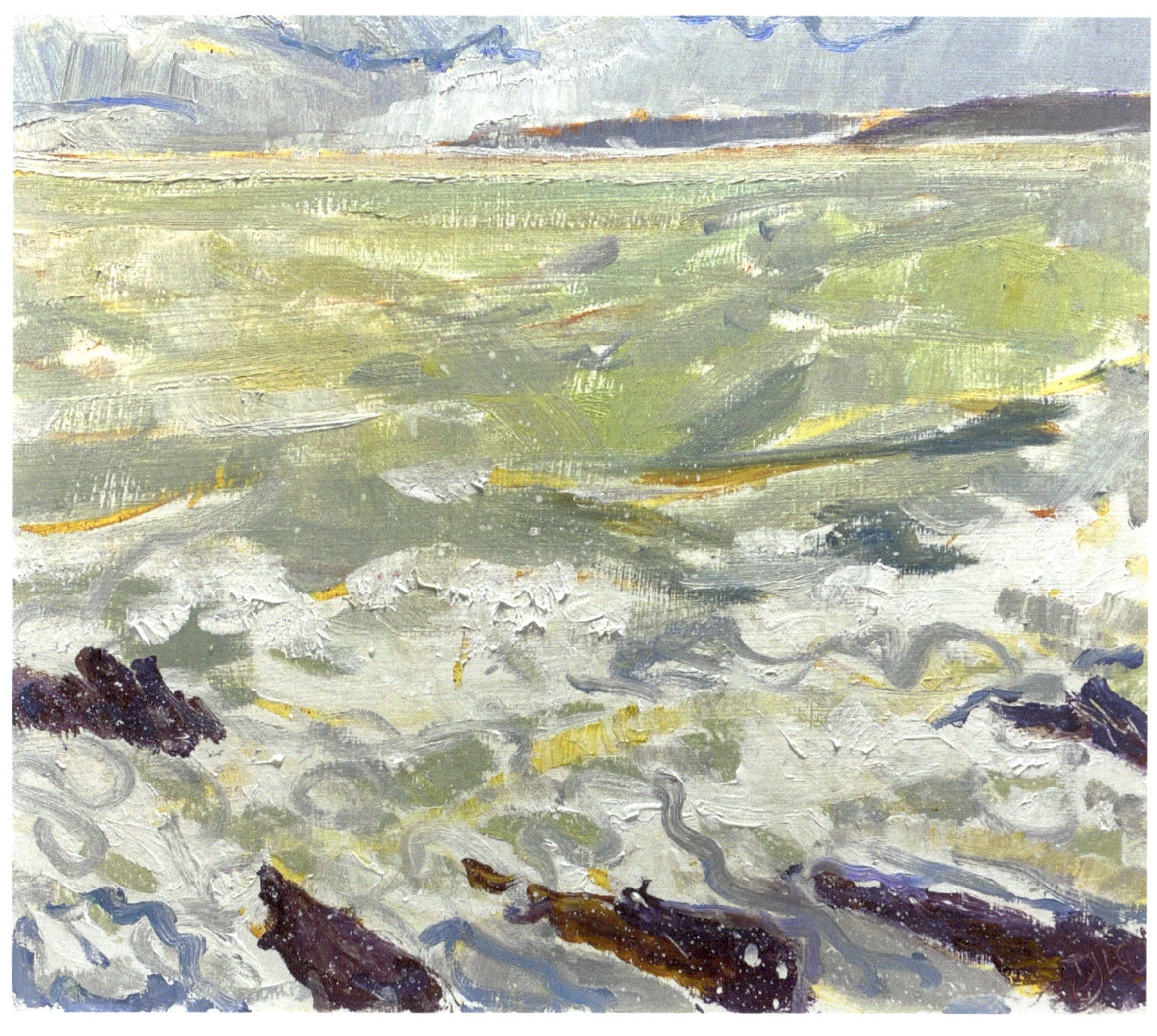

31/12/22
Final Pier House and Project Painting
/// spill.elaborate.output

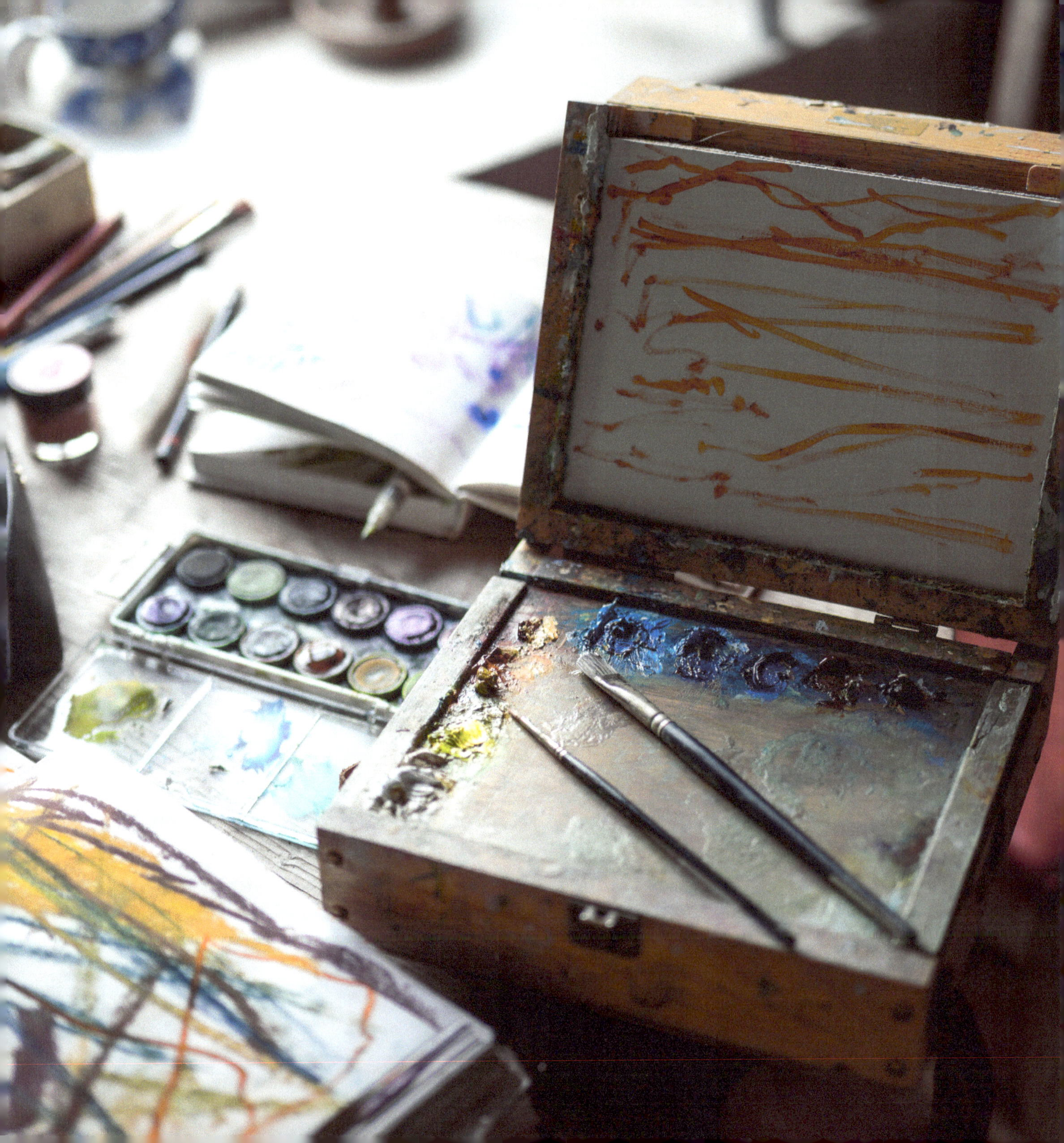